T0160787

Discipleship Style Coaching

Discipleship Style Coaching

Helping Others Cross the Secular-Sacred Divide

DR. JERRY BREEDLOVE, JR.

Carpenter's Son Publishing

Discipleship Style Coaching

©2019 by Jerry Breedlove

All rights reserved. No part of this book may be reproduced or transmitted in any form or by any means, electronic or mechanical, including photocopying, recording or by any information storage and retrieval system, without permission in writing from the copyright owner.

Published by Carpenter's Son Publishing, Franklin, Tennessee

Published in association with Larry Carpenter of
Christian Book Services, LLC
www.christianbookservices.com

Scripture quotations marked (ESV) are from the ESV® Bible (The Holy Bible, English Standard Version®), copyright © 2001 by Crossway, a publishing ministry of Good News Publishers. Used by permission. All rights reserved.

Cover and Interior Design by Suzanne Lawing

Edited by Gail Fallen

Printed in the United States of America

978-1-949572-45-2

About This Book

Assisting others in the process of leadership development comes in many forms. In recent years, coaching has continued to grow as a popular way to accomplish this, which has catalyzed the emergence of different models. What follows is the exploration of one such model the author terms "discipleship style coaching" (DSC). The DSC model is a distinctly Christian model of coaching that intentionally embraces the principles of Christian discipleship and blends them with coaching methodologies. This blending of coaching and discipleship is intended to help both professional and amateur Christian coaches as they seek to advance a culture of coaching in the many organizations in which they have influence. According to the author, this can be accomplished in formalized coaching engagements as well as in informal ones spanning a variety of organizations as small as family units to small businesses and nonprofits, even to multibillion-dollar corporations. One of the most unique aspects of the DSC model is how it can help leaders at all levels cross the ever-increasing divide between the secular and the sacred in order to bring the principles of the kingdom of God into the places where Christians live, work, and play. Using both scholarly research and relevant examples, the author unpacks how the DSC model can be used to transform individuals, organizations, and ultimately whole communities.

Contents

Introduction

As he was getting into the boat, the man who had been pos-
sessed with demons begged him that he might be with him.
And he did not permit him but said to him, "Go home to your
friends and tell them how much the Lord has done for you,
and how he has had mercy on you." And he went away and
began to proclaim in the Decapolis how much Jesus had done
for him, and everyone marveled.
(Mark 5:18–20, English Standard Version)

Mark 5:18–20 seems like a strange way to begin a book intended to help business leaders, pastors, parents, and coaches assist people across the ever-widening chasm between the secular and the sacred—what I term the "secular–sacred divide." However, the principle in this passage serves as the impetus for such a noble initiative.

Before we determine how to help others in this way, and even before we decide if the intersection between coaching and discipleship I propose is a viable vehicle for such help, we must determine if Jesus had such "chasm crossing" in mind. That is, did Jesus intend for us to take the message and hope of the gospel—the good news of the kingdom of God—into the world in such a way? Or, instead, did he believe that we should simply build church programs and outreach efforts that seek to draw men into the church? Should Christian men and women primarily build a sacred institution where people can come to learn about Jesus, or should they focus on developing and mobilizing a force of missionally minded believers who cross into the secular realm (the realm of business, politics, sports, entertainment, etc.) in order to bring gospel influence into every facet of life?

These are tough questions. They are questions that defy simple Sunday school answers. They are questions that drive us directly to the heart of the Christian faith and, admittedly, they are questions that have been answered by the previous generations of faithful men and women of the church. However, they are also questions that must be addressed adequately and answered by the current generation of believers in ways that both remain faithful to scripture as well as provide specific answers to the context in which we live.

This book provides nothing that is genuinely new to the conversation surrounding the divide between the secular and sacred, nor is it my claim that it even provides new information on how best to cross this divide. Rather, this work provides a new lens through which we can look at age-old principles and apply them in ways that both make sense and are effective. This book stands on the shoulders of the faithful cloud of witnesses described by the author of Hebrews (Heb. 12:1–2) and the subsequent generations of believers who have sought to live out their calling as salt and light in a world desperately in need of such preserving agents (Matt. 5:13–16).

Intrigued? Then read on. But beware. The lens this book uses has the potential to cause a paradigm shift in your thinking so profound it will change the very fabric of our society. If the status quo is something you are comfortable with, this may wreck you for Jesus as it challenges long-held assumptions about the nature and role of disciples of Christ. I hope you can find beauty in that wreck, just as the demon-possessed man did when he crossed the secular-sacred divide.

CHAPTER 1

Wrecked for Jesus . . . and Then Sent Home

And he did not permit him but said to him, "Go home to your friends and tell them how much the Lord has done for you, and how he has had mercy on you." (Mark 5:19)

Much has been written about the events of Mark 5:1–20. This passage has been instrumental in informing the church in multiple areas of doctrine and practice. The doctrine of divine healing and suffering has been shaped by Jesus' touch on this man. Also, the imperative to take the hope of the gospel to non-Jews has also been explained and reiterated by this and similar passages and many other doctrines as well. However, sending this new Christian away has only been briefly touched upon by most scholars. Why did Jesus send the man away after healing him? Why not let him come along with the rest of the disciples to sit at his new master's feet and bask in his glory? This question touches the very heart of the gospel.

Noted theologian and author N. T. Wright argued that sending away this former demoniac had a specific kingdom purpose. No longer was this man to rely upon Jesus in the way he had already experienced; instead, he was to learn to trust Jesus in a new way. This way was to return to the community that had once ostracized him. He was now to stand upon his own two feet, in a new life, and tell his non-Jewish people (the secular world) about all that Jesus had done for him.

Please do not allow the enormity of this to escape your notice. Jesus had followers who dogged his heals from town to town, but he sent this man immediately back across the secular–sacred divide in order to influence the broader world with the hope of the kingdom of God. He did not say, "Yes, I think it would be a grand idea if you stayed close to me for the next several years learning everything you can and, then, maybe when you are ready, I will send you back to your people." Instead, Jesus said, "Go home to your friends and tell them how much the Lord has done for you, and how he has had mercy on you" (Mark 5:19b). This does not mean that there is not a time or place for being discipled in more traditional ways already familiar to those within the church. Rather, it points to the fact that the primary mission of God was to influence the broader world—not just those who had been redeemed. Upon further scrutiny, the passage also reveals another truth.

Jesus did not simply send back an envoy to this people. He sent them one who the passage clearly indicates they were not comfortable with. In fact, the whole incident engendered fear within the population of this area. Jesus had effectively made a further wreck of this man's life by increasing their derision toward him. However, Jesus was unwilling to allow their fear, speculation, and confusion to push away the very thing they needed. Instead, this man's testimony would be a critical part in reaching the people and teaching them to live by kingdom principles. This concept is radically different from the regular experiences of modern communities of faith. To understand this, most people need only to think of their personal testimony of coming to faith in Christ.

MY PERSONAL STORY

During my six-month overseas deployment to the country of Kosovo, the September 11 attacks occurred against the World Trade Center in New York City. Upon my return in November 2001, I was immediately scheduled to make a second foray into the hostile territory of Afghanistan. However, God had other plans. While deployed to Kosovo, the communications terminal I operated for US military forces had missed a critical system upgrade, and we were pulled from the mission at the last possible moment. This seemingly random event would be the start of something dramatic in my life.

While I was in Kosovo, my wife had been invited to a local church as part of their outreach program. She had decided she would try it out, but she also decided not to commit long term to the church because she was uncertain of what my reaction would be. To her surprise (and even mine), after returning from Kosovo, I agreed to begin attending the church with her. However, the deployment to Afghanistan threatened to end this tenuous exploration of the Christian faith, and this is likely why God directly intervened. By missing the deployment, I was able to continue attending weekly services at this church, and in April 2002, I gave my life completely and totally to Christ.

The rush of new life that Jesus provided was amazing. I was eager to help others experience the same and asked my new pastor for guidance. Instead, he encouraged me to reach out to my friends and bring them to church so that *he* could begin to teach them about Jesus. I do not blame him for this approach, because it was the only one he had been taught. But can you see the issue? I had effectively been wrecked for Jesus; had a strange new outlook on life; and had my friends, coworkers, and family scratching their heads in dismay.

My pastor did not say, "Go home and tell everyone what the Lord has done for you." Instead, he gave me a list of super-cool events that I could bring people to, events where they could begin to explore the faith. I am not saying these events were a bad idea. As a matter of fact, several of my friends and coworkers began to attend the church with me. Some of them even gave their life to Christ as well.

But I have often wondered: What if, after Jesus had caused this beautiful wreck in my life, my pastor had helped me discover how I could reach my own friends with the hope of the gospel? What if, rather than doing all the work himself, my pastor had taken time to coach, disciple, and develop me on how to bring the kingdom principles I was learning into everyday use where I lived, worked, and played? How many more might have come to know Christ? How many countless thousands might be members of the family of God if the command had been "go" rather than "stay"?

Again, I do not blame my pastor. He was and is a godly role model who was simply doing ministry the way he had been taught. This way, however, only served to increase the gaping chasm I call the secular–sacred divide. The longer I was in the faith, the more I stayed on my side of the chasm. Once-friends turned into acquaintances, and acquaintances slowly became nothing more than silent memories. What's more, I began to struggle with questions of how I could effectively bring my faith into my workplace, neighborhood, and places where I used to hang out. My former friends felt the changes too.

Men and women with whom I had once been close came to see me as a stranger in their midst. Some even became fearful of my newfound faith. Others took it upon themselves to try and win me back over to their side of the chasm. This only caused me to increase my efforts to ensure I stayed firmly rooted on my side of the divide. I began to strategize bigger, more creative ways where I could lure my friends to cross this increasingly effective barrier to the gospel. Don't miss that. My expectation was that *they* would be the ones to do the work to cross the divide. Rather than me going to them, they would need to come to me to see what, if any, difference the Christian faith could make in their lives. It was not until God called me to plant a church that things would begin to slowly change for the better.

The First Church Plant

Approximately one year after I became a Christian, the Lord called me to plant a church. This never ceases to amaze me, because I was so young in the faith. But then I remember this was not the first time Jesus had done such a drastic thing. Remember, the demoniac Jesus had healed was only a believer for a few short hours before he sent him out with a similar assignment. This is because planting a new church is not so much about forming an organization as it is about taking the hope of the gospel to a group of people who might not otherwise experience it. This was especially true in my case.

The tribe I am affiliate with, the Christian and Missionary Alliance (C&MA), did not have a group of people who were clamoring for a new church to be planted. As a matter of fact, most people in the community viewed our church-planting efforts with skepticism—sometimes even with antagonism. This meant for me, and the small team I was working with, that we had to cross secular-sacred divides by going to the places where people lived, worked, and played.

My first step in this was to secure employment with a major retailer in one of their distribution centers. While this assignment was one of the toughest I have ever experienced, I am grateful that the Lord pushed me across the divide in the same way he did the former demoniac. During my two years of employment, I became known throughout the facility as "the floor-line preacher." This was because my job in industrial maintenance allowed me ample opportunity to work alongside people who were busy throwing freight on conveyor systems. As I got to know these people, I found that it was often natural to bring up things of the faith. Much of this I credit to my spiritual gift of evangelism, but I still wonder if I would have been able to reach more people if I had someone who would have coached me on my regular encounters with people on the other side of the divide.

I can specifically remember one lady (and her boyfriend) who I would talk to. I thought things were going well; however, I later learned they had lodged a complaint against me to senior management for harassing them with my Christian faith. I was shocked—even a little angry—that this would happen. It caused me to scale back my efforts at crossing the chasm for a while. This did not mean I quit altogether. I was confused about how I was supposed to be able to continue being effective in sharing my faith at work without putting my secular job in jeopardy. This is a common issue among many believers.

After two years of working outside the church, the Lord opened the door to be in paid, full-time ministry with our church plant. I leapt at the opportunity knowing this was the next thing he had for me, and the lessons I learned while working in the secular world would be helpful as I worked with others facing similar dilemmas. Up until this point, I had never heard of coaching, and I certainly had no idea of how to blend coaching principles into a robust model of discipleship. Most of the work I did with parishioners was in the form of encouraging them (sometimes driving them) to swallow their fears and just share Jesus. Lots of beautiful wrecks happened as people encountered Jesus, but a lot more ugly train wrecks happened.

The bad wrecks kept happening because I was in unchartered territory. None of the people in my circles were experienced in how to help people cross the secular–sacred divide. Instead, they (like my former pastor) had been taught the way to influence the world for the gospel was to have really cool events that were so fabulous people could not possibly stay away. Of course, we all knew this was not really effective because we had read the book of Acts. We saw that what we were doing was not getting anywhere near the same results as the early church. But in our ignorance, we simply chalked it up to a problem with society.

While all this was going on, I kept being told by those in the C&MA I served under that we were having phenomenal results compared to what others were experiencing. Our little church plant that started with nine people had grown to over 350 and had become the flagship church in our region in many ways. However, I knew in my heart something was wrong.

At a national gathering of C&MA churches, I would do something drastic. In a moment of courage, I approached the chairman of the board of my denomination and asked him if he would be willing to coach me. I did not even know what coaching really was, I just knew that it was synonymous with help—and help was what I needed. To my surprise, he agreed, and we began a coaching relationship that spanned many years. This first taste ignited a passion in me for coaching that I still have today. It has been instrumental in bringing me to this point in my journey where I now blend coaching principles with the familiar principles of discipleship.

The Second Church Plant–Replanting an 80-Year-Old Congregation

One of the most powerful lessons I learned from my first coach is that the coach did not always have the answers. That was as it should be. The coach's purpose was not to fix all my problems. The coach's role was to help me reframe my current reality and develop a plan to achieve my desired goals, which was a radically different thought process from the discipleship model I had been taught. In traditional discipleship models, I learned the leader was supposed to be the one with the answers, and it was his or her job to teach those answers to one being discipled. The disciple's part was to figure out how to apply the answers I provided. The change my coach introduced, though, would be an integral part of my learning—one that was especially important in my second church plant, because some of the problems I encountered baffled even him.

In 2010, the Lord called my family to move from Tennessee—a place that had become home—to western Pennsylvania. We were getting an opportunity to replant a church that was over 80 years old in the heart of a sleepy little college town. As we accepted this assignment, I was excited about the possibility of reaching college students for Christ, equipping them to integrate their faith into their chosen field, and sending them out as missionaries *of sorts* after graduation. What I did not understand was the remnant of people remaining in this church had other plans.

Upon arriving in Pennsylvania, my family quickly learned that the people who had called us to help them replant this once-thriving church now on the verge of closure were completely uninterested in crossing the secular–sacred divide. I distinctly recall a conversation with one prominent member who told me that the church was a place to shelter away from the world, and if "those people" wanted to join us they would have to first clean up their acts. I did not let this deter me. I worked extra hard to model the kind of Christian walk I wanted to see from them. I also regularly consulted with my coach who helped me frame new goals and behaviors. In the end, the bulk of the already small group I started with decided to leave the church. However, we had started reaching some college students, and they were hungry to learn how to live their faith out day to day. This was the first true experience I had where I was intentionally blending discipleship and coaching with people who were trying to cross the secular–sacred divide.

I am thankful for those relationships I was a part of then. Those students, and eventually some adults, put a great deal of trust in me as I started getting my coaching legs under me and blended coaching principles into my discipleship process. I am honestly not sure why (other than God's favor), because I barely knew what I was doing coaching. But God honored it, and the students became increasingly effective at incorporating their faith at school and work. However, not everyone was impressed.

My coaching extended to some adults as well. In particular, one of my female staff members was being coached regularly as part of the discipleship process with her. As she applied our coaching sessions, she came up with a radical idea. Just a few miles away from our church was a night club where exotic (i.e., naked) dancers performed. My staff member did the unimaginable and began an outreach to these ladies. I was so excited by this I could scarcely believe it—nor could some of the church members. One of my church elders came to me and said his wife could never help this woman do that outreach because it would defile her (i.e., the elder's wife). Did I mention this elderly saint was blind? Yes, a blind, God-fearing, elderly saint (I have no doubt she is a born-again Christian) said she would be defiled if she reached across the secular–sacred divide. This extreme example taught me that I had more to learn about how to disciple people if they were ever going to be the ones to cross the chasm and influence the world with the gospel.

The good news is that God honored my efforts, the church tripled in size, and it is still growing under the current pastor there. This was despite all the mistakes I made, not having answers that seemed to help some people, and losing most of the core group that started the work with me. It was then that I transitioned to the only fully established church I have ever led.

The *Healthy* Church

About three years into my tenure at this church I was replanting, my regional team leader asked if I would consider pastoring a church about 45 minutes away. He said they were looking for a leader just like me—someone strong and out of the box—to help them move to the next level in their ministry. For my second interview with them, I showed up on my motorcycle wearing a t-shirt, ball cap, jeans, and tennis shoes. I walked into the meeting, put my feet on the table (theirs were on the table as well), and said, "I came like this today because I do not want to 'date' you guys. Instead, I want to show you who I really am and let you make whatever decision you think best." I think they were shocked, but they hid it well.

Over the course of a couple of months of interviewing, we finally decided it was the right fit for my family, and we accepted the call to lead this congregation. The church surged under my leadership, and we rapidly began talking about how to accommodate all the people. The first year seemed to be going great, but there was a sinking feeling inside of me. I realized for the first time as a pastor that I had planted myself firmly back on the sacred side of the divide. I literally did not know (really know) a single person in the town who was not a Christian at the church I was pastoring. Therefore, all my talk about crossing the secular–sacred divide was falling on deaf ears. Something had to be done.

I talked to my coach about this. He challenged me to come up with some way to get connected to people in the community. Finally, I decided the best course of action was to join a local bowling league. I was an awful bowler, so I joined the Bad Bowlers League at my local alley. Through this league, I started making connections with the community. Eventually, some of the people from my church joined as well. From there, I decided, with the help of my coach, to get better at bowling and volunteer as an assistant coach for the middle school and high school bowling teams of our town. This turned into me getting certified as a bowling coach and later earning the bronze-level certification with the U.S. Bowling Congress. Through these efforts, people started coming to faith in Christ. What was even better was that people inside the church started wanting to reach across the secular–sacred divide as well. The growth at the church, in my opinion, was wonderful, and most of the congregation agreed. However, there were a few *power brokers* who did not. This is when the trouble began.

I vividly remember one unmarried couple who had come to Christ via bowling and started attending the church. They were loving what was happening in their lives, and it was such a great testimony to how my coach had helped me reach back out across the secular–sacred divide. However, one day they simply disappeared.

When I tracked them down, I was shocked to learn why. They told me the people at church did not want them. I argued this was not the case, but they were convinced. In a moment of transparency, they confessed to me that they had been approached by multiple people at the church and told they should stop attending until they were married. The reason? They were living together in sin; this meant they were *playing* church. People told them God was not impressed and wanted them to quit attending until they changed. I was devastated. Could this really be happening? It turned out that it was, and it was the beginning of the end of my time with this church.

Over the next several months, I learned that multiple people who I, as well as others, had crossed the secular–sacred divide to reach were being intentionally chased out of the family of faith. This was used to undermine my credibility as a leader. It was not long before everyone within the church who I was coaching and discipling one on one was being viewed as an enemy by the power brokers I mentioned above. Even worse than that, I had recently started expanding my coach/discipler efforts to help people in the church in their business pursuits. Now, because my credibility was shot, those sessions slowly ground to a halt.

Though it pains me to admit, I did not handle this new reality with grace. I began lashing out at different leaders and finished what they had started for them. It appeared that crossing the secular–sacred divide could quickly undo my leadership in the church. My coach helped me through this. Ultimately, we discerned together that my time there was drawing to a close, which brings us to the present day.

The Current Church Plant

My time in the previous church was the closest I have ever come to quitting in all my years of ministry. For about a year I was miserable where I was serving. Though I was well compensated (one of the best paid in my region), I could not stand what I was doing day in and day out. This is when a series of events led me to uproot my family and move to the Kansas City metropolitan area to plant our current church, and we decided we were going to plant this new church with some major intentionality.

Right away we recruited other like-minded believers to move to KC with us. Multiple families ultimately uprooted and moved to a strange new city because they believed, as do I, that crossing the secular–sacred divide was not only doable, it is what God requires of us. All of the core members of the team, including me, work full time in the business (secular) world. Some work in retail, others sell insurance, others labor in factories, some teach school in the public schools, and I (you guessed it) coach executives full time. Our church is growing, albeit slowly right now, in a healthy way. We do not throw a lot of big events meant to attract Christians from other churches. Instead, we all reach out to the unchurched and unsaved through our workplaces, places we play, and neighborhoods.

I still bowl, coaching leagues for youth and sometimes adults. I even got a part-time job coaching a high school team. What is even more amazing, I coach senior managers and executives who are members of some of the most successful companies in our city, and a lot of times I get the chance to disciple them as well. Not only that, I coach the men and women of the church plant, helping them discover how they can continue crossing the secular–sacred divide. Not all of these coaching and discipling relationships are perfect. Sometimes they are far from it. However, I feel good because I am back to practicing what I preach.

I believe Jesus longs to see his people cross the secular–sacred divide on a regular and consistent basis. I believe by crossing that divide myself as I coach to business leaders, kingdom principles are slowly and steadily permeating the landscape of our secular culture. Finally, I believe that by coaching, discipling, and encouraging others as they do the same, we will see a lasting legacy in heaven.

In the next chapter, I unpack how the intentional blending of coaching and discipleship works. I teach the principles of good discipleship style coaching (DSC) as I know them, and I share my own successes and failures to help you learn. However, I want to make something clear. My goal is *not* to help anyone become the best coach, discipler, or leader. Being a great helper to those with whom you interact will be a byproduct of my real goal. My true goal is to wreck your theology, your conceptions of God, even your methods of advancing the kingdom, and then send you home like the demoniac of Mark 5 to tell others all that the Lord has done for you. Then I want to help you explore ways in which you can disciple and coach others to do the same in order that the kingdom of heaven might fully come.

---

1 Wright, N. T. (2004). *Mark for everyone*. London, England: Society for Promoting Christian Knowledge.

2 McFadyen, P. (1997). *Open door on Mark: His gospel explored*. London, England: Triangle.

3 Collins, G. R. (2002). *Christian coaching: Helping others turn potential into reality* (2nd ed.). Colorado Springs, CO: Navpress.

CHAPTER 2

The Nature of the Discipleship Style Coaching Relationship

And they came to Jesus and saw the demon-possessed man, the one who had had the legion, sitting there, clothed and in his right mind. . . . [Jesus] said to him, "Go home to your friends and tell them how much the Lord has done for you, and how he has had mercy on you." And he went away and began to proclaim in the Decapolis how much Jesus had done for him, and everyone marveled. (Mark 5:15a, 19b–20)

Admittedly, there is not much—in the way of quantity—we can glean from Mark 5:1–20 on the process of discipleship style coaching (DSC) and how it applies where we live, work, and play. However, the quality of insight that comes from this short passage is another thing altogether because it deals with the nature—the very heart—of the process itself. What, then, does this passage reveal about the nature of the blending of coaching and discipleship? To answer this question, we must first label the insights in ways that make sense to modern men and women. Then we can explore them more in depth.

While not completely evident at first glance, this passage reveals three major truths about coaching that all discipling coaches must know. The first is that coaching is a form of positive psychology that helps generally healthy people (e.g., emotional and spiritual health) move further into the positive by enhancing the well-being and performance of the individual being coached.[1] This seems incredible to say, especially considering the individual used as an example was demon-possessed just hours before, but it is true nonetheless. The second is that coaching is less concerned with the coach giving detailed instructions to the coachee on what the best goals are to pursue and the most effective pathway of pursuit. Instead, it assumes that the coachee is resourceful and creative and promotes the coach discovering with the one being coached what the best way forward is rather than dictating the path for the coachee.[2] Finally, it helps reveal that it is the coachee who takes responsibility for the outcomes, while the coach provides accountability, encouragement, and support; serves as a sounding board; and even delivers *tough love* at times.[3]

As mentioned in the previous chapter, this is different than what most of us have experienced in more traditional discipleship models. In those models, Bible study of topics or passages chosen by the discipler is the primary means of helping another grow. R. A. Torrey wrote,

> *There is nothing more important for the development of the spiritual life of the Christian than regular, systematic Bible study. It is as true in the spiritual life as it is in the physical life that health depends upon what we eat and how much we eat. The soul's proper food is found in one book, the Bible.[4]*

While Bible study is certainly an extremely important part of the discipleship process, this quote underscores an unstated, but heavily implied, basic set of assumptions. First, it assumes the newfound disciple is malnourished, generally unhealthy, and needs to be nursed back toward health by a steady diet of the word. Second, it implies the scriptures are detailed instructions for living the Christian life that should be taught via the leader's agenda for the disciple rather than being a sacred text from which generally healthy people can and should draw principles for living from in order to continue growing healthier as they encounter life's various obstacles. Finally, it places responsibility for the spiritual growth of the disciple on the leader instead of on the disciple while the leader encourages and holds the disciple accountable.

These conclusions may appear to be somewhat of a stretch at first. However, if we observe the discipleship process of the majority of churches, these underlying assumptions become evident. One way we can see this is to peruse the Christian bookstore's discipleship section. As you do this, look closely at the discipleship materials offered, especially the leader guides for the various studies. When you open a leader guide, chances are you will find detailed descriptions in each section on what the learning outcomes are supposed to be. A study on stewardship will perhaps have a lesson on helping people understand that everything we have belongs to God. This, in and of itself, is a great Christian principle Christ followers should learn. However, the lesson's placement in relation to the other lessons indicates *when* the disciple should learn it, and the process of learning described in the leader guide for the lesson describes *how* the disciple should learn it.

Although it is not the intention of such studies, I have found in my ministry that study leaders often fret over how they are going to achieve the outcomes the lessons set forth.

This happens so much that it becomes increasingly difficult to find men and women willing to assume leadership because they cannot accomplish the goals set forth in leader guides. Do not misunderstand me. I am not saying these types of studies are inherently bad. I am simply trying to convey how the studies unintentionally exploit a significant flaw in many discipleship models. They place the agenda and responsibility on the leader rather than on the disciples because they assume disciples are not healthy enough to know on their own what they need to learn. While this is sometimes the case, thus giving these types of studies a legitimate place in discipleship models, it is my conjecture this is true far less often than we assume.

This is why I propose a different set of three principles on which to build a discipling model, which I term discipleship style coaching (or DSC) and sometimes simply call "discipleship" and at other times "coaching." Within my own church, I most often refer to this model as "spiritual formation"—an intentional language change with my congregation that makes us question why, what, and how we disciple others. No matter which term I use, what I mean is DSC, unless I specifically state otherwise. Let us now turn our attention to where these principles are specifically derived and how they apply in DSC.

PRINCIPLE 1–POSITIVE PSYCHOLOGY AND GENERAL HEALTHFULNESS

The first principle of DSC revealed in the Mark 5 passage is that it is rooted in positive psychology; at the same time, it goes beyond its scope. As modern research on coaching has grown, much of this has been conducted by positive psychology practitioners. This is because positive psychology focuses on issues of happiness, well-being, and progress toward ever-increasing positive goals.[5] The practice of coaching shares many of the same underpinnings as this field because its focus is primarily on helping the coachee to move forward from a place of general healthfulness (i.e., mental, emotional, and spiritual) into increasing health as the coach and coachee focus on positive outcomes instead of remedying dysfunction. This is not to say that coaching never addresses negative behavior. It means that the primary focus of the coaching relationship is to assist a reasonably well-adjusted individual in the pursuit of positive goals. This is why coaching, while sharing roots with positive psychology, is not simply another form of counseling. This is also why it is important for DSC practitioners to have some level of familiarity with counseling and psychology.

This familiarity is needed so that a discipling coach can see when the model is not appropriate with a particular individual. In the case of the Mark 5 demoniac, Jesus did not encourage a sick man to go out and pursue his dreams. Instead, the Lord first ensured this man had the proper healing he needed from those negative mental, emotional, and spiritual issues that were holding him back. For Jesus, his omniscience enabled him to know exactly what this man needed healing of and how to heal it. Not until the man was "in his right mind" (Mark 5:15b) did Jesus send him across the secular–sacred divide.

Before the second and third principles of the model can be implemented, the foundation of a generally positive state must be established. For many discipling leaders, this involves developing a high level of self-awareness and discernment to know when a potential disciple should be referred to other professionals (i.e., counselors, psychologists, or doctors) for help before coaching can begin. An example will help illustrate how this is done.

Renee's Story

Renee was an executive coaching client I was working with as she was making a transition in her career. She had been previously employed by a large multinational corporation as a director in a profitable division. A series of unfortunate events had caused Renee to lose her position at this company. After months of searching for a job without any results, Renee turned to career transition coaching for help.

Over the first several appointments, we explored her professional background, crafted a new resume, and began developing strategies that would help her find a perfect position. However, it began to appear that Renee was self-sabotaging her career search. In one coaching session, she broke down sobbing and opened up to me about several old wounds that were keeping her from effectively pursuing her goals. As I employed every coaching technique I knew, it became apparent that Renee was still haunted by demons from her past that I was not equipped, as a coach, to help her deal with. At this juncture, I had a choice. Do I continue coaching her in hopes I could help her land a job, or do I need to refer her to a professional counselor better equipped to deal with the matter? The answer was obvious.

During the latter half of the coaching session, I asked Renee if she thought getting the help of a professional counselor would help. As Renee contemplated this, she concluded it would. Others at my company were initially surprised when they learned that I had placed coaching with Renee on hold while she got help. However, I knew—as did she—that she was not in a generally healthy place to move forward with the coaching process. Thus, I referred her to a licensed professional counselor. Although I do not know what happened with Renee in her sessions with the counselor, after about a month she was ready to resume her career search. In short, I guided her to the help she needed so that when we resumed our coaching she would be, like the former demoniac of Mark 5, in her right mind, on positive footing, and ready to move forward. A short time after, Renee found her a new position, one in which she is still serving and thriving today.

The choices I made regarding Renee were not easy. My income is primarily derived from my executive coaching practice, and here I was turning a client away. However, I knew that my training, the coaching literature, and the scriptures all supported the idea that coaching can only be effectively and safely accomplished with those who are generally healthy.[6] This means the only ethical choice I could make was to refer the client to those who could help and then resume coaching when she was in a better place.

PRINCIPLE 2–THE DISCIPLE IS IN CONTROL OF THE PROCESS

The second principle revealed in this passage that goes to the very heart of DSC is who is in control of the session agenda. It would appear, at first glance, that Jesus was the one in control of setting the agenda for the man seeking his aid. This is because the man initially wanted to go with Jesus, sit at his feet for learning, and continue to draw strength from Jesus (the coach in our scenario) as he faced new challenges. In response, Jesus told him no, suggesting that he return to his own people and share with them all that Jesus had done for him in order to advance the kingdom of heaven. However, Jesus was not setting the goals for this man's life, nor was he prescribing a certain process he needed to follow to reach those goals. Instead, Jesus was refusing to bend to an unhealthy agenda this man initially had.

In effect, Jesus told the man, "Your initial agenda is not a healthy agenda because it will make you dependent on me in ways that you should not be. Instead of pursuing life in this overly dependent way, let's try something different." Jesus employed this same principle regularly as evidenced by his use of parables and stories as recorded in the gospel records. The storytelling that he did was powerful in helping those who sought him to define goals, including the steps toward those goals, without manipulating the hearers. This is a skill that it is critical for discipling coaches to develop[7] However, this begs the question: How can someone become overly dependent on Jesus?

The short answer is that the man's initial plan was to be a passive recipient of Jesus' teaching (a more complete answer is explored in the third principle). Jesus, though, was not seeking people to be passive recipients. Instead, he stood ready, willing, and able to come alongside those who were ready to cross the secular–sacred divide. The former demoniac was one such man, although he did not yet know how to do this. Jesus helped him by refusing to be manipulated into an unhealthy agenda. Coaches can and should give gentle nudges toward healthy goals (or away from the unhealthy) without prescribing specific courses of action.

It would be intriguing if Mark had included the rest of the conversation Jesus had with the man. We might learn what this man's specific process for reaching his own people was. However, in God's infinite wisdom, this is not recorded for us. We are simply told that he went back to his people and proclaimed what Jesus had done, and the people were greatly influenced in a positive way for the kingdom of God (Mark 5:20). This allows readers to reasonably conclude the man was largely responsible for deciding the specifics in his course of action. The coachee was in control of the agenda, while the coach provided support in discovering the best way forward.

It is important to point out that the formerly demon-possessed man was not forced by Jesus to return to his people. It was his personal choice whether or not to follow this advice. One only need look to the story of the rich young ruler recorded in Mark 10:17–22 to discover that people can and do resist crossing the secular–sacred divide—even when Jesus is the one prompting.

Kevin's Story

In the early days of my coaching people who were attempting to cross the secular–sacred divide, I noticed a startling trend. People who had experienced Jesus radically invading their lives, wrecking and remaking their worldview, and then prompting them to go share with others what he had done tended to gravitate toward a stance of wanting to simply stay with Jesus in the relative safety of the church walls. Oftentimes, this would manifest as the individual sharing with me that he or she was called into full-time Christian service as paid staff of whatever church I happened to be leading. There were many more people *volunteering* to come on paid staff than we had money to support, so it was easy to tell them that this was impossible. Looking back, I think God placed limits on those funds in order to ensure I figured out how to best encourage people to cross the secular–sacred divide. Eventually, however, the ministries I led grew to a level where multiple staff could be financially supported, and this is where Kevin's story comes in.

Prior to coming to saving faith in Christ, Kevin had lived a rough life filled with drugs and crime. When Kevin was a convicted felon sitting in a jail cell, he came to know Jesus as Lord. After getting out of jail, Kevin decided to follow Jesus by ministering to youth. During the early years of this, Kevin supported himself and his family as a carpenter (a little ironic, I know). Eventually Kevin's carpentry job would cause him to relocate to the town where I lived, and the family found a church home where I was serving.

As I got to know Kevin, we eventually decided I would begin discipling him as he pursued the best ways to take the hope of the gospel across the secular–sacred divide. The longer we journeyed together, the more Kevin pushed to be hired as full-time staff at the local church. His reasoning was that he could serve the Lord more fully if he didn't have to work a secular job. I challenged these thoughts, gently pushing back in order to help him shape his future goals. Eventually, Kevin decided to leave the church in pursuit of a position as a church planter in a large city. Our DSC continued, and Kevin continued to frantically search for ways to get out of the secular work world and into full-time ministry. Eventually, Kevin left the church plant to pursue a position in youth ministry with a church he believed would soon be able to pay him to serve in the church full time.

As of this writing, he is still not employed full time by the local church—although he receives a paycheck from them for two days of work per week. Kevin is still trying to figure out how to get into full-time ministry because he is convinced he can do so much more if he can cross the secular–sacred divide in order to reside fully in the sacred realm. No amount of assistance, to this point, has helped Kevin see that being sequestered within the church walls will help his ministry flourish. On the contrary, the more Kevin takes the gospel into the secular world, the more fruit he bears. However, Kevin is in control of the agenda, and I have tried to help him shape goals and design a plan of action to reach those goals. I believe Kevin is somewhere between the ends of the spectrum of the rich young ruler (who chose to ignore Jesus) and the demoniac (who chose to heed Jesus). As a discipling coach, I find this is most often the case. Disciples of Christ are usually somewhere on a sliding scale, and the leader's job is to help them discover where they are, where they want to be, and how to move toward that goal.

Charles' Story

The story of another man I helped serves to illustrate even more clearly how the coachee is in control of the agenda, goals, and pathway to action and why this is so important. Charles was a mid-senior finance executive with a multibillion-dollar domestic company. During our coaching, Charles had decided he wanted to pursue a new career in a different company. As we worked together to flesh out what the process would look like, Charles and I often had differing opinions. Many of our differences came from Charles wanting to pursue strategies that I had repeatedly seen fail for other clients in similar situations. However, as the coach, my job was not to get him to follow my advice. My job was to help him figure out the best pathway forward for him and help him implement it.

As his career transition dragged on, Charles encountered other issues in his life that interfered with the goals he had set. The career transition was on again and then off again for several months, but one day Charles called with some news. He had participated in a first interview with a company he thought might be a good fit. Naturally, I was excited for Charles. We explored what we could on this company. As we dug into the history and background of the company, we discovered a large portion of the revenue was derived from providing payday loans and check cashing services. As a believer, I was instantly concerned this may be a bad fit for Charles. As a Christian, Charles also had reservations about working for a payday lender because of the potential for predatory lending.

During our next coaching session, I brought up my concerns to Charles in such a way to intentionally shift from typical coaching into DSC. He listened attentively and developed a plan to vet the company to ensure they were not involved in immoral, unethical, or abusive practices with their clientele. During the vetting process, Charles discovered from multiple reputable sources that this company was one of the most well respected in its industry. In fact, the federal and state government had used this company as an example for similar ones on how to engage in payday lending that was not considered predatory. This discovery eased my concerns. More importantly, it proved that Charles was correct in setting the goal and subsequent strategy for pursuing employment with them. Charles was the one who felt he should cross the secular–sacred divide into this industry and eventually help kingdom principles take hold in it.

As of this writing, Charles is still employed with this company in a high-level position, and he is influencing the payday lending industry in positive ways that reflect kingdom values. I shudder to think what would have happened if I had tried to take control as the coach, and I am thankful to God that—in his sovereignty—Charles was able to cross the secular–sacred divide in ways I never would have fathomed.

PRINCIPLE 3–COACHEES DO THE WORK, COACHES SUPPORT

The final principle derived from the Mark 5 passage that is supported in the coaching literature is that the coachee implements the goals set inside the coaching process. The coach's role is to support, which includes accountability, encouragement, resourcing within reason, and (in the case of Christian coaches) prayer. That the coachee is the one who does the work is clear from Mark 5:20 in which we discover it is the former demoniac who proclaimed in the Decapolis the good news of what Jesus had done in his life. This same man is the one who reaped the rewards of the people being smitten with the kingdom of God. This revelation is underscored by what is revealed in Mark 5:21.

In Mark 5:21, readers discover that after sending the man back to his own people to pursue the fruits of crossing the secular–sacred divide, Jesus got back in his boat and went to a different region to work with different people. This fact is repeated over and over again as Jesus helped various people in pursuit of their kingdom purposes. Jesus was constantly coaching, discipling, guiding, empowering, and then *releasing* people to go and achieve their God-given dreams. In the effort of individual people who have been empowered by God, the kingdom advances across the secular–sacred divide.

This principle is not intended to suggest that what the discipling coach provides for the client is not work. In fact, the discipler does his or her fair share of the work in the first two of the three phases of the DSC process. In Phase 1, the initial steps of the engagement, the leader is responsible for much of the work in building the relationship with the coachee (or disciple). Without this relationship, the intervention is unlikely to succeed. In Phase 2, necessary support, the coach facilitates ongoing learning for the coachee and provides adequate support to achieve his or her goals. However, in Phase 3, ongoing efforts, it is the coachee who provides the effort to implement and sustain the desired changes.[8] While these phases appear to make coaching (even DSC) look like a linear process, the reality is that they overlap and are deeply interconnected parts of the overall process. Another example from the life and ministry of Jesus serves to illustrate this point.

Jesus Sends Out the 72

In the Gospel of Luke, Jesus had been working closely with a group of 72 people on crossing the secular–sacred divide. He built relationships with them via the initial phase, provided necessary developmental support for them as Phase 2 overlapped Phase 1, and then sent them out to enact ongoing efforts.

> *After this the Lord appointed seventy-two others and sent them on ahead of him, two by two, into every town and place where he himself was about to go. And he said to them, "The harvest is plentiful, but the laborers are few. Therefore pray earnestly to the Lord of the harvest to send out laborers into his harvest. Go your way; behold, I am sending you out as lambs in the midst of wolves. Carry no moneybag, no knapsack, no sandals, and greet no one on the road. Whatever house you enter, first say, 'Peace be to this house!' And if a son of peace is there, your peace will rest upon him. But if not, it will return to you. And remain in the same house, eating and drinking what they provide, for the laborer deserves his wages. Do not go from house to house. Whenever you enter a town and they receive you, eat what is set before you. Heal the sick in it and say to them, 'The kingdom of God has come near to you.' But whenever you enter a town and they do not receive you, go into its streets and say, 'Even the dust of your town that clings to our feet we wipe off against you. Nevertheless know this, that the kingdom of God has come near.' I tell you, it will be more bearable on that day for Sodom than for that town." (Luke 10:1–12)*

The individuals who went out and did the work of the kingdom were those Jesus had discipled, coached, and developed. Jesus also crossed the secular–sacred divide himself by continuing his work; however, those Jesus had developed were given the freedom, encouragement, and empowerment to implement their own goals and strategies. The process did not stop at this point. Jesus' disciples returned to him to debrief the experiences they had and receive further assistance from him as a discipling coach (Luke 10:17–20). In this follow-up session, Jesus provided ongoing support, accountability, and encouragement as the men and women he had developed shared with him their successes and failures, and this is important, as you will see.

The people we help, like those Jesus helped, will inevitably suffer setbacks from time to time as they seek to cross the secular–sacred divide and bring kingdom principles into their realms of personal influence. One poignant example comes from Mark 9, where Jesus' disciples had been out working and failed to help a young boy who was demon possessed. In a private session with Jesus, the following exchange occurred: "And when he had entered the house, his disciples asked him privately, 'Why could we not cast it out?' And he said to them, 'This kind cannot be driven out by anything but prayer'" (Mark 9:28–29). In this instance, Jesus had actually helped his disciples by demonstrating for them how they could accomplish their goal (i.e., he delivered the boy from oppression). Then he helped them reframe their failure by pointing out why it had not succeeded. This was only possible because he had engaged in all three phases in a continuous, overlapping basis with them. What is more exciting is that for those of us who have read the New Testament, we find that the men and women Jesus assisted continually increased in their abilities to bring kingdom realities to their people— something Jesus predicted would happen if they stayed the course. "Truly, truly, I say to you, whoever believes in me will also do the works that I do; and greater works than these will he do" (John 14:12a).

Larry's Story

One man I employed DSC with for many years has experienced coaching to this degree. When Larry and I first became involved with one another, it was on a church planting team where I served as his pastor. Larry was a drunk and a drug addict who had come to church in a last-ditch effort to save his marriage. Shortly before we began working together, he had given his life to Christ, but he had not been able to progress much further in his journey past getting saved. The first year of our time together involved an awful lot of me trying to *fix* my friend—like he was some sort of project. Yet, the more I grew to know Larry, the more I genuinely cared about him. As our relationship grew, I began to see this man differently.

The first major shift happened in *my* thinking—not his. I began to see him as a generally healthy person. I stumbled into the first principle of coaching with him that I could apply to our discipleship process—I shifted from a negative view to a positive view. After this shift in my viewpoint, I began to trust him to develop and control the agenda of where our times together would take him. This meant Larry could focus on the things that were truly important to him, rather than me interfering with what I thought was most important. As this happened, goals and strategies developed, enabling Larry to cross the secular–sacred divide and bring the kingdom of heaven to his secular workplace, his hobbies, and even his family. Because I did not know how to address the issues in his life, he was forced to participate in deeper ways in his own progress. This caused him to have to do the work himself, and it allowed me to revel in providing support, accountability, and encouragement as he did. In the end, the transformation in his life was so dramatic that people who had previously despised this man came to love him.

After several years, Larry had grown so much in his ability to influence others for the kingdom of God, our times shifted away from his personal development into helping him learn how to employ DSC with others. I wish I could say this was intentional on my part, but it was not. God, in his sovereignty and grace, had brought to me a man to disciple who desired to reproduce the results he had accomplished in others. To this day, Larry's efforts in helping others and advancing the kingdom have far surpassed my own. And I am more than OK with it! It is something I marvel about on a regular basis.

Throughout the remainder of this book on using DSC to help people to cross the secular–sacred divide, I use the example of Larry and me to unpack what DSC means, as well as provide a model for how you can achieve similar results with those you are working with. I hope that our story of DSC, how Jesus wrecked Larry and then sent him home, will help you to see how you can apply this new model to get similar results.

Are you ready to keep learning?

---

1 Palmer, S., & Whybrow, A. (Eds.). (2008). *Handbook of coaching psychology: A guide for practitioners.* New York, NY: Routledge.

2 Kimsey-House, H., Kimsey-House, K., Sandahl, P., & Whitworth, L. (2011). *Co-active coaching: Changing business, transforming lives.* Boston, MA: Nicholas Brealey.

3 Stoltzfus, T. (2005). *Leadership coaching: The disciplines, skills, and heart of a Christian coach.* Virginia Beach, VA: Coach22 Bookstore LLC.

4 Torrey, R. A. (1906). *How to succeed in the Christian life.* New York, NY: Fleming H. Revell Company, p. 46.

5 Gold, J. (2012). *A natural alliance: Positive psychology, hope theory, and executive coaching* (Order No. 1516361). Available from ABI/INFORM Collection, pp. 20–21.

6 See Palmer and Whybrow's (2008) work on coaching psychology for a fuller treatment of this subject.

7 Reissner, S. C., & Angélique, D. T. (2011). Power and the tale: Coaching as storyselling. *The Journal of Management Development, 30*(3), 247–259.

8 Smith, A. T. (2012). Middle grades literacy coaching from the coach's perspective. *Research in Middle Level Education Online, 35*(5), 1–16.

CHAPTER 3

Is This a Believer-Based Discipleship Model or Something More?

For it will be like a man going on a journey, who called his servants and entrusted to them his property. To one he gave five talents, to another two, to another one, to each according to his ability. Then he went away. . . . Now after a long time the master of those servants came and settled accounts with them. . . . His master said to him, "Well done, good and faithful servant. You have been faithful over a little; I will set you over much. Enter into the joy of your master."
(Matt. 25:14–15, 19, 21)

Different leaders and coaching professionals have observed that the discipleship style coaching (DSC) model involves many time-tested discipleship techniques. While this is true, I believe this model goes beyond Christian discipleship into a way to influence the larger world with Christian principles. I conclude this for many reasons, and Renee's story serves as one example why. The reason Renee's story is such a poignant example of this being more than discipleship is because Renee is not a Christian. As a matter of fact, Renee is a highly agnostic individual.

Let this sink in for a moment. As a coaching professional, I have brought kingdom principles into Renee's life in order to help validate the gospel message to her. More than this, though, the model I propose for DSC has enabled me (the Christian coach) to faithfully proclaim Christ to people who might not otherwise have a chance to believe. Don't miss this important point! The method of DSC I am engaged in is not only helping people like Larry cross the secular–sacred divide, it is also providing a pathway for discipling coaches such as you and me to cross the same secular–sacred divide on a regular basis. This begs the question: Does this model always work for crossing the secular–sacred divide and influencing the world in a positive way for the kingdom of God?

The answer to this question is complex. In many ways, it *is* always successful as long as the coach is faithful in his or her attempts to discern where, when, and how to insert kingdom principles into the DSC relationship. However, it is *not* always successful in bringing people to a saving knowledge of Jesus Christ, nor is it a guaranteed way to ensure obedience to Christ and Christian principles for those who are already believers. If this is the case, then why use this model at all? Why not keep searching for a model that works flawlessly every single time? The answer is simple yet as profound as the gospel itself. It is built upon Christian principles that have been applied to kingdom work in various ways throughout the centuries—though it has not been historically labeled as DSC.

As discipling coaches, it is not our responsibility to ensure everything goes right every single time. Instead, as the parable of the talents (Matt. 25:14–30) helps us understand, our job is to be faithful with those things we have been entrusted with. In our case, it is being faithful to our role as a coach by being there for the people we are coming alongside of, offering support, encouragement, and activities that help them reframe their particular situations and move forward in positive ways. However, as N. T. Wright so astutely pointed out, Christians often view the parable in question as a sort of story to indicate there is a heavenly examination we are preparing for while we walk on this earth.[1] This feeling that everything is a test causes many people to operate in a type of fear, and this fear often causes us to second-guess ourselves.

For the sake of argument, let us assume the parable of the talents is about a test of some sort we are taking. In the parable, the master told the servants who had taken a chance and actually used the talents that they had done well and were considered faithful. The servant who was condemned was not condemned because he lost the master's money—he actually had lost nothing. He was condemned because he did not try to accomplish anything with the resources he had been entrusted with. It was not about flawless execution, it was about whether or not the servant took a faith-filled risk to advance the kingdom of heaven here on the earth. This should free us to take risks with ideas, programs, and even models that do not always work.

Furthermore, the improvement of any coaching model, including the DSC model, can only come by testing the theoretical basis for the model with actual real-world applications. This provides an answer to the question: Why not continue searching for a model that works flawlessly every time? If we are continuously engaged in deploying the DSC model outlined in this work, we will accomplish kingdom work along the way. Ultimately, this work will include further refinements to the model and strategies of implementation I will share. Before I share the model, though, it would be good to take time to reflect on the last statement. This model is not the definitive model of coaching and discipleship Christian leaders should utilize. Rather, it is a starting point for discipling coaches meant to help you and me as we strive to grow better at our craft.

THE MENTAL MODEL FOR COACHING ACROSS THE SECULAR-SACRED DIVIDE

The first step in becoming effective at DSC, which attempts to move across the secular–sacred divide, involves the intentional development of a new mental model. Mental models enable individuals to develop a conceptual thought process about how things work in the real world.[2] At times, mental models can cause organizations and individuals to fall into patterns of behaviors that are less than idealistic; however, mental models can also be highly effective tools used to intentionally shift paradigms and explore new possibilities.[3] Thus, mental models should not be seen as static, rigid, or even unchanging mental constructs meant to flawlessly guide discipling coaches in their everyday practices. Rather, mental models should be seen as fluid and changeable approaches meant to enable people to see possibilities, understand how things work together, and empower discipling coaches and coachees (disciples) to move forward effectively in the DSC process. The mental model for coaching across the secular–sacred divide that is outlined below is no exception.

What, then, is the mental model for DSC aimed at helping individuals across the secular–sacred divide? This six-point model borrows heavily from both the models of coaching as well as the numerous models of Christian discipleship, and it is rooted and grounded in the Judeo–Christian scriptures and worldview. My conceptualization of these points, outlined and briefly described, are explored more in depth in subsequent chapters and are supported from both the discipleship and coaching literature as well as from broader support from Christian authors and theologians. The six points are as follows.

1. Everyone is a potential coachee or disciple (e.g., paid coaching clients, bosses, subordinates, peers, family, congregation members, and even friends).

2. Effective DSC involves extensive prayer (sometimes the coachees are actively involved in the praying and sometimes they are not).

3. Coaching and discipleship are best accomplished by skillful listening and questioning (only sometimes does coaching involve intentional training and/or giving advice).

4. Coaching and discipling agendas and goals are set by the coachee, not the discipling coach.

5. DSC is effectively accomplished by applying the GROW framework for coaching.

6. DSC involves intentional coaching and discipling encounters (most often those encounters are scheduled, but sometimes moments are simply seized).

Everyone Is a Potential Disciple Who Can Be Coached

The first point of the mental model for coaching across the secular–sacred divide is concerned with shifting the paradigms held by potential DSC leaders. This is true for those who are officially called coaches as well as those who simply wish to use DSC principles in their many relationships. For many coaches and leaders, coaching principles are only intentionally applied to those interactions where there has been some type of agreement (formal or informal) that the relationship will be one of coaching. Coaches are limited to applying coaching techniques with people who have agreed to be coached. While it is appropriate to rely on coaching techniques and principles for these types of relationships, coaching can also be effectively applied with bosses, peers, coworkers, family members, friends, neighbors, subordinates, and practically anyone. This is especially the case when coaching moves away from more traditional secular models of coaching and into DSC.

The major mental shift that must occur for discipling coaches is embracing the idea that coaching principles are an effective form of influence one can use in a variety of relationships—often much more effectively than other forms of influence. This is because coaching, when done well, is not about telling people what they must or must not do but about helping others discover the best ways forward in whatever situations they are facing. This mental shift, when accomplished, opens the DSC practitioner up to a world of possibilities where he or she can perfect the art and craft of DSC.

Effective Christian Coaching Involves Extensive Prayer

Prayer is part and parcel to an effective, happy, productive Christian life. Both the scriptures and the historic witness of the Christian church has repeatedly demonstrated that prayer is the work of God's people in both a public and private setting.[4] Many authors, Christian thinkers, theologians, and pastors have even argued prayer is *the* primary work of the people of God and a foundational discipline on which the church is grown and strengthened.[5] However, the use of prayer in coaching has often been limited or overlooked, especially when coaching those who are not Christian.

To consistently cross the secular–sacred divide, Christian coaches must incorporate prayer into every DSC encounter and relationship. Often this crossing is accomplished by prayer with coachees, especially when they are willing to allow Christian principles to be openly applied to the coaching relationship. However, the coach's prayer life *for* his or her coachees (even without their knowledge) opens the world of DSC to new and magnificent possibilities, some of which might even include non-Christian coachees coming to a saving knowledge of Jesus Christ. This is because intentional prayer with and for others invites the Holy Spirit to influence the situation in profound ways as the discipling coach declares his or her dependence on God.[6]

Coaching and Discipleship Are Best Accomplished by Skillful Listening and Questioning

To effectively employ the previous point of the mental model for DSC that aims to cross the secular–sacred divide, discipling coaches must be highly skilled listeners adept at asking appropriate questions to coachees deeper into the DSC process. Simply asking good questions in DSC encounters is not enough. These questions must also be well timed and go directly to the heart of the matter at hand. This is only accomplished as the discipling coach learns to effectively listen. Listening involves not only listening to the coachee or disciple but also to the still, small voice of the Holy Spirit as he guides the discipling coach.

Agendas Are Set by the Coachee/Disciple–Not the Discipling Coach

Closely related to DSC involving intentional encounters is

the idea that coaches—not the discipling coach—set the agendas for such times. This does not mean discipling coaches are not co-creators of the agenda within sessions. It means that leaders, whether professional coaches or simply leaders using DSC principles in their regular interactions, allow and even encourage the coachee or disciple to take the lead in defining what areas are important to him or her. Allowing the coachee to take such a lead role is a catalyst for making the person feel important and cared for as the issues he or she is currently facing are those being addressed. While coach-directed training and development activities do have their place in the DSC process at times, this should not be the primary method for developing session agendas.

DSC Is Accomplished by Applying the GROW Framework to Encounters

Next, any coaching model, traditional or discipleship style, must use an effective framework to guide the individual encounters and overall relationship. Though simple, I have found the GROW framework to be effective. GROW is a simple acrostic that helps the discipling coach ensure essential steps in coaching are covered. G is for goals, which reminds the coach to help the coachee to set goals that he or she can aim for. R is for reality, which prompts discipling coaches and coachees to objectively look at where the coachee is at in any given situation. O is for opportunities or obstacles, and it helps coaches to remember that with any goal one is trying to achieve there will be opportunities and obstacles that must be adequately addressed for the coachee to reach his or her goal. Finally, W is for way forward. Thinking of the way forward helps coaches and coachees effectively design actionable steps the coachee will follow to achieve the goals.

DSC Coaching Involves Intentional Encounters

Most, if not all, coaching or discipleship practitioners realize these activities must involve intentional encounters. This is true for the DSC model as well, and it often occurs as individuals schedule regular appointments to meet with the discipling coach, complete assignments between appointments, and interact with the discipling coach on an as-needed basis between scheduled appointments. However, in the mental model for DSC aimed at crossing the secular–sacred divide, highly impactful encounters can be seized by the discipling coach as often as they are planned. These seized opportunities can occur at places like the family dinner table, the Bible study or a Sunday school classroom, a barbecue, a sporting event, or even a casual walk.

The point of this list is not to limit when and where DSC can take place, nor is intended to undermine what organizations like the International Coach Federation have done to define and shape the coaching industry.[7] Rather, it is intended to help a discipling coaches make the mental shift that effectively helping others with the DSC model can (and often does) occur in the most mundane of settings if he or she is willing to actively search out those opportunities and ultimately create a culture of DSC inside of every organization (formal and informal) they are part of.[8]

I have found that many of the most impactful coaching times I have been involved in were not the scheduled DSC sessions but when I was able to discern the opportunity to intentionally coach or disciple someone in an unplanned, unscheduled interaction. However, seizing DSC opportunities should not be done simply for the discipling coach to advance his or her own growth as a DSC leader. It is only appropriate to do such when it is in the best interest of the one being assisted as the discipling coach attempts to function as a servant leader modeled after Jesus' life and ministry (Matt. 20:28; Mark 10:45), which naturally leads to the next shift in the mental model needed for coaching across the secular–sacred divide.

The Mental Model Is Not Rocket Science

The mental model I propose is actually quite simple in its basic concepts. However, it takes time working with the model to learn how to employ it effectively in DSC relationships. At times I have been guilty of making the model more convoluted than it needs to be, which has served to confuse the DSC process in those instances. When the process described, whether with an individual or group, has not been going well, it has been helpful to reflect on the mental model I propose to ensure I am not making it overly complex. Often, this is exactly what has happened, and simplifying my approach has helped to get those DSC relationships back on track.

In the next six chapters, we explore in depth each of the six points in the mental model. This exploration includes both the theoretical basis for each of the points of the model, as well as real-world examples of how the model has been effectively employed. My hope is that you view this model as simple enough that you have confidence you can remember it and employ it effectively. At the same time, I hope you learn the model is robust enough that it can be effectively used to cross the secular–sacred divide and bring kingdom principles into the places where we live, work, and play.

---

1 Wright, N. T. (2004). *Matthew for everyone, part 2: Chapters 16–28*. London, England: Society for Promoting Christian Knowledge.
2 Brewer, W. F. (2001). Models in science and mental models in scientists and nonscientists. *Mind & Society*, 2(2), 33–48.

3 Mandal, A., Howard, T., & Antunes, D. (2009). Dynamic linkages between mental models, resource constraints and differential performance. *Journal of Strategy and Management, 2*(3), 217–239.

4 Bullock-Webster, G. R. (1912). Intercession. In G. Harford, M. Stevenson, & J. W. Tyrer (Eds.), *The prayer book dictionary*. New York, NY: Longman.

5 Schemm, P. R. J. (2012). The writing pastor: An essay on spiritual formation. *Themelios, 37*(3).

6 Ryken, P. G., & Hughes, R. K. (2005). *Exodus: Saved for God's glory*. Wheaton, IL: Crossway Books, p. 462.

7 See https://coachfederation.org/core-competencies for the core competencies set out by the International Coach Federation.

8 Crane, T. G. (2017). *The heart of coaching: Using transformational coaching to create a high-performance coaching culture* (4th ed.). San Diego, CA: FTA Press.

CHAPTER 4

Every Relationship Has DSC Potential

Go therefore and make disciples of all nations, baptizing them in the name of the Father and of the Son and of the Holy Spirit, teaching them to observe all that I have commanded you. And behold, I am with you always, to the end of the age.
(Matt. 28:19–20)

It may seem a stretch to some readers that the basis for the first shift in our mental models of coaching, every relationship has the potential to become a coaching relationship, being based on a command from Jesus to disciple all nations. The strangeness of this may even be compounded further by my assertion in the previous chapter that coaching is more than another form of discipleship. However, there is a sentiment dwelling at the heart of the Great Commission (Matt. 28:19–20) that transcends discipleship. It is the idea that every human being we encounter has inherent value, the ability to grow, and the hardwiring from God to do just that. This, I know, is a bold statement and one worth exploring. If correct, it has the ability to transform how we view others and our responsibilities toward them.

THE PASSAGE EXPLORED

One noted Christian thinker, theologian, and author remarked of the Great Commission, "The tasks Jesus leaves his followers, tasks which will bring his sovereign authority to bear on the world, are straightforward enough to outline, though daunting and demanding to put into practice."[1] The first of these tasks, making disciples of all people, is the focus of our current exploration. Of this passage, John Calvin is known to have explained that the commission delivered by Jesus was for his followers to expand the gospel's impact everywhere—in every arena of life.[2] The very idea of *every arena of life* means Christian men and women will actively have to seek to cross the secular–sacred divide in order to enter those areas currently closed off to the gospel. These are areas such as the business world, secular government, the education system, and others that seem nearly impervious to Christian influence. This is especially true in America, where the current interpretation of the separation of church and state is increasingly viewed as a de facto ban on Christian influence being exerted anywhere outside of the four walls of the church's facilities.

When the world is increasingly closed off to the gospel's influence in such ways, how are we to effectively bring kingdom principles to bear? I believe a large part of the answer is by Christians engaging in discipleship style coaching (DSC) activities with every man, woman, and child they encounter. We must intentionally employ the DSC model to cross the secular–sacred divide.

Some, however, might argue the imperative to make disciples of all nations is aimed at growing Christian converts in their faith and knowledge of Jesus Christ. While this certainly is a part of the Great Commission, it is unlikely Jesus meant solely this. For instance, the Greek word we translate into "make disciples of" in this passage is *methēteusate*—a transliteration of the word into English characters—which carries the meaning of instructing someone in the ways or teachings of a specific teacher or leader. The argument can be made the *someone* in question is he or she who has already come to Christ for salvation. However, Johannes Louw and Eugene Nida made a compelling argument that the language likely means "convince them to become my disciples or urge them to be my disciples."[3] Their argument is supported by Christ's assertion that this is to be done with "all nations," which has historically been understood to mean all people groups we come in contact with, including those who do not yet believe. The question is not actually one of who we should attempt to influence for the kingdom but *how* we best go about this.[4] One version of the *how*, DSC, is the subject of this book.

This does not mean that the *what* of our teaching is unimportant. On the contrary, a strong argument can be made that it is not simply facts about Jesus and his teachings people should be learning. Obedience to those teachings—actual application to life situations—is what Jesus intended. This is shown by Jesus' instruction to teach them—the people we are influencing for the gospel—"to observe all that I have commanded you" (Matt. 18:20). Observation, in this context, is not simply keeping watch and remembering. It is observing by obedience to and active participation in the principles Jesus taught.[5]

When the Great Commission (Matt. 28:19–20) is understood in this way, it leads to a single, logical conclusion. Those who profess to know Christ as Lord must actively seek to influence others for the kingdom of God by teaching them about Christ, his teachings, and other kingdom principles. In the process of spreading this influence, Christians are to target both those inside the church and those outside the church. To do this, they must intentionally cross the secular–sacred divide. The chief aim of this influence is so Christian principles will be applied and obeyed in all areas of life. This cannot be accomplished unless we view all people as potential disciples of Christ. This is where the difficulty of old mental models arises.

THE OLD MENTAL MODEL

In Kansas City, the wonderful area of the country where I now reside, there is a current debate happening among church leaders regarding the idea of how to best address missional barriers. Missional barriers are things that block the advancement of the gospel occurring either naturally (i.e., language, culture, age, gender, etc.) or happening mentally (i.e., they are not like me, I am not smart enough, I have not been a Christian long enough, etc.) or are created by our process (i.e., they have to come to church to hear, they have to convert first to be taught, it is not safe to mingle with non-Christians, etc.). Current Christian leaders in this city are assigning an M-number for each barrier that prevents the advancement of the gospel and kingdom principles for the particular contexts. Figure 1 represents how this might look, including the orbit in which the church typically functions.

Figure 1. M-numbers for each barrier that prevents the advancement of the gospel and kingdom principles.

In M0 relationships, the people are generally the same as me. They are at about the same socioeconomic level, the same race, same gender, close in age, operating in the same stage of life, and similar in other such ways. In M1 relationships, one of these items is different. For instance, an older, white, English-speaking male in a middle-class family might be seeking to influence a young adult male in the same background. However, M2 might mean there is a different race for each person as well as different age; M3 could introduce a third variable of different socioeconomic standing with the other differences; M4 could introduce a different a gender difference; and M5 and beyond introduce other differences as well. A study of the churches showed that Christians continuously operate in spreading the influence of the gospel only in their M0 and M1 orbits, and very few, if any, churches had people attempting to make a kingdom impact in relationships at the M2 level and beyond. However, in these same churches, it was discovered that the vast majority of the people had extensive, regular interactions with people at the M2 level and beyond. Why are so few people attempting to influence others for the kingdom outside of the M0 and M1 orbits? I believe this is happening because of our old mental model.

In the old mental model, the one we are trying to shift, we do not view people at the M2 level and beyond as being influenceable. We do not view every person we come in contact with as a potential disciple of Christ. When confronted with this truth, people push back and say, "That is not true. They can be influenced for the kingdom. It just needs to be someone who is a little more like them to be able to do it effectively." This is precisely where the new mental model of viewing every relationship we have as a potential DSC relationship can have such power.

DISCIPLESHIP STYLE COACHING INSTEAD OF SIMPLY DISCIPLING

The primary difference between coaching and Christian discipleship is who makes the move into the other person's orbit. In discipleship, we most often expect the disciple to do the work of crossing the missional barriers of gender, language, ethnicity, and other barriers to enter the orbit of those in our church in order to begin to learn about Jesus and start following him. However, if Christian culture of DSC is to be developed, the opposite must be true. The discipling coach must do the hard work of crossing the barriers to influence the other person with kingdom principles.

I am certain I am not the first coach or disciple maker to have observed this, because it has been strongly implied in the many books and countless articles I have read on coaching and discipleship. However, I have never seen it explicitly stated in the way I have done. The fact it has not been explicitly stated before does not lessen the credit the statement should be given. In all instances of successful DSC, the discipling coach does the work of crossing over into the other person's orbit to help him or her define their goals, take stock of their current reality, identify the opportunities they have and the obstacles they must overcome, and then develop a set of actionable steps to achieve those goals. What keeps us from doing this effectively and regularly?

The short answer is it is hard work. It is not easy to enter into another person's world, gain understanding of their situation from their perspective, and then help them move forward in the goals they want to achieve. Beyond the hard work, it is also psychologically uncomfortable because the discipling coach is constantly required to suspend his or her personal beliefs and biases. But is the hard work and discomfort we feel really reason enough to hold back? If we want to be able to say with integrity we are taking the Great Commission seriously, it is not.

The command from Jesus was for the Christian to go and influence others, urging them to become his disciples and teaching them to obey the things he taught. The Christian is to be salt and light in a lost and dying world (Matt. 5:13–15). The Christian in the relationship is required to see the potential in the other person and then help that person tap his or her potential to become all that God has designed him or her to be. The Christian is who must be the servant in the relationship, just as Jesus came to serve and not to be served (Mark 10:45). This can only happen if we intentionally begin to shift our mental model and see every relationship we have as a potential DSC relationship where kingdom principles can be brought to bear on every situation our friends, coworkers, family members, and neighbors face. Larry's story helps illustrate why this mental shift is so important.

Larry Came to Jesus—But It Wasn't Enough

In the summer of 2002, Larry's marriage and personal life were in serious trouble. Larry had been consistently working to climb the corporate ladder in the building materials industry as a high-level sales professional. He was making money hand over fist, and his increased affluence served as a catalyst for a rather lavish and reckless lifestyle. To grow his business, his professional role required him to work long hours on job sites engaging contractors, and it often meant many after-hour engagements where he would wine and dine his clients in order to grow relationships. This lifestyle eventually led Larry to a dependence on drugs and alcohol and a tendency to leave his wife and children at home, leaving them to care for their own personal and emotional needs. As with many ill-adjusted people, Larry and his family also engaged in an ever-increasing form of *retail therapy*, where they sought to buy happiness and life fulfillment by accumulating expensive boats, cars, trucks, and other such things in their lives. This led Larry and his wife to a place where they had no choice but to file personal bankruptcy. The added stress further strained a marriage already at the breaking point. Larry eventually separated from his wife in preparation for divorce.

One day, as Larry was on his way to work, he noticed a church sign advertising a series of sermons on growing a healthy marriage. In a moment of desperation, he turned to the church to see if it was possible to save his failing marriage. His wife reluctantly agreed to give it another shot, and they began attending the church. In a relatively short amount of time, the pastor of the church paid Larry and his wife a home visit. During that visit, Larry gave his heart and life to Christ and became a Christian. The pastor and church members celebrated this victory and encouraged Larry and his wife to enter into regimented program of discipleship to grow in their newfound faith.

Interestingly enough, the church followed the marriage series of sermons with a series on biblical stewardship of personal finances. Larry and his wife gobbled this teaching up. Rather quickly, they engaged in the Christian practicing of tithing their income—giving one tenth of their income to the local church in honor of God and to support the ministry. However, the church's program of discipleship was lacking because, while it was teaching biblical principles to its members, the teachers were not attempting to cross into students' worlds on how best to apply those principles in every area of life. This disconnect caused Larry and his wife to misunderstand major parts of the biblical principles of stewardship and tithing, and they began engaging in a series of *giving events* where they attempted to bribe God.

Larry and his wife thought all they had to do to have more was to give more. Thus, their lifestyle did not change, lavish spending continued, substance abuse ran rampant, and the family rapidly returned to a place where they were living far beyond their means. They amended the bankruptcy claim from restructuring their debt under a Chapter 13 bankruptcy to a Chapter 7. All the while, the church leadership (including the pastor) were blissfully unaware of the extent of the hardship for this family.

Why was all of this occurring in this way? A large part of the answer is that Larry and his wife were separated by missional barriers, as described in Figure 1, from the majority of the congregation. Those barriers included things such as the drug and alcohol use, the income level of the family as compared to the rest of the congregation (Larry earned nearly double that of the average congregation member), Larry and his wife's marriage was his second (the congregation was vocal about divorce and remarriage being sin, placing divorcees in a different class of people), and other such things. Larry and his wife were required to do the work of crossing the missional barriers, and they accomplished this by hiding those aspects of their lives from the church family that did not comport with the church norms. In short, Larry's eternity in heaven had been secured while his life continued to spiral out of control.

About this time, I met Larry as I began attending his church and ultimately became the associate pastor of the congregation. In what can only be viewed as the providence of God, I felt a calling to plant a daughter church of this congregation, and Larry's family believed God wanted them to be a part of the church-planting team with us in a neighboring community. I was not, however, prepared for what was about to happen.

Our church-planting team was small—only nine people. This allowed my wife and me to have ample time to spend with Larry and his wife in order to get to know them on a deeper level. As we came to know them, my wife ultimately started providing daycare services for their family. One day, after Larry came by to pick up his kids, he was involved in a car accident close to our house. The accident itself was relatively minor considering he rear-ended a woman in her car at a stoplight. However, Larry was initially in such distress about the accident that we thought someone had died. As we talked with him about what happened, we quickly learned everyone was fine. This led me to curiosity as to why he would be so upset. Curiosity, as we explore later, is a key component discipling coaches should not ignore.[7]

As I questioned Larry about why he was so distraught about the accident, he shared about his drug use—as recent as the day before—and the insistence by the company he worked for that he immediately submit to a drug test. This revelation was startling for two reasons. First, I realized I had done a less than acceptable job of crossing over into Larry's world in order to influence him for the kingdom. Here was a man who had at least one area of his life he was keeping secret from me as I intentionally discipled him in the Christian faith the way I had always been taught. Second, I was taken aback due to the overwhelming sense I had that helping Larry was going to involve a set of skills I did not then have.

The discipleship processes the church had engaged in with Larry and his family had never sought to help them cross the secular–sacred divide with their faith. Church was church, and the rest of life was the rest of life. In other words, this family was living highly compartmentalized lives, compartments this family actively sought to keep separate from one another because they saw no way for kingdom principles to be applied outside of church life. Larry was saved by grace for sure, but this was as far as it went.

I thank God for the accident Larry had on that fateful day because it made me keenly aware something was wrong with the mental model I had about influencing others with kingdom principles. I saw Larry as a disciple, one who was created in the image of God and had inherent value, a person who had the ability to grow, and one who was hardwired by God for growth. What I had not seen up until the accident was that this growth should be happening in every area of his life. The accident, and its revelations, caused me to respond in new and different ways to Larry based upon the realization I needed to work much harder at entering his world instead of forcing him into mine. The drugs and rampant spending were just the tip of the iceberg. Over the many subsequent years fumbling through learning how to apply DSC principles in our relationship, I found Larry's life was largely untouched by kingdom principles. The good news is God was present, and he helped me shift away from typical forms of discipleship into a more robust DSC relationship with Larry. It literally changed his world and mine.

---

1 Wright, N. T. (2004). *Matthew for everyone, part 2: Chapters 16–28*. London, England: Society for Promoting Christian Knowledge, p. 207.

2 Calvin, J., & Pringle, W. (2010). *Commentary on a harmony of the evangelists Matthew, Mark, and Luke*. Bellingham, WA: Logos Bible Software.

3 Louw, J. P., & Nida, E. A. (1996). *Greek-English lexicon of the new testament: Based on semantic domains* (2nd edition.). New York, NY: United Bible Societies.

4 Cabal, T., Brand, C. O., Clendenen, E. R., Copan, P., Moreland, J. P., & Powell, D. (2007). *The apologetics study bible: Real questions, straight answers, stronger faith*. Nashville, TN: Holman Bible Publishers, p. 1461.

5 Utley, R. J. (2000). *The first Christian primer: Matthew* (Vol. 9). Marshall, TX: Bible Lessons International.

6 Manser, M. H. (2009). *Dictionary of Bible themes: The accessible and comprehensive tool for topical studies.* London, England: Martin Manser.

7 Stoltzfus, T. (2005). *Leadership coaching: The disciplines, skills, and heart of a Christian coach.* Virginia Beach, VA: Coach22 Bookstore LLC.

CHAPTER 5

Discipleship Style Coaching Must Involve Extensive Prayer

I appeal to you therefore, brothers, by the mercies of God, to present your bodies as a living sacrifice, holy and acceptable to God, which is your spiritual worship. Do not be conformed to this world, but be transformed by the renewal of your mind, that by testing you may discern what is the will of God, what is good and acceptable and perfect. (Rom. 12:1–2)

Perhaps these two verses seem like an odd way to begin a discussion about the need for extensive prayer in a discipleship style coaching (DSC) model, seeing that there is no direct reference to prayer or even any form whatsoever of the word pray. However, it is my intention to demonstrate how this principle outlined in this pericope directly links to prayer and informs the practices of the proposed model of DSC. The key to gaining this understanding lies within grasping what it means to experience transformation via the renewal of one's mind and subsequently learning to train our powers of discernment.

THE PASSAGE EXPLORED

To understand the gravity of what Paul is instructing Christians to do, it is important to look closely at several of the words Paul chose in the original language. First, the words "I appeal to" are translated from the Greek word *parakaleō*—a transliteration of the word into English characters. This word carries with it a sense of begging, urging, or beseeching.[1] Paul emphatically asked his readers to pay close attention to his instructions here. These instructions are extremely important for the proper functioning of the Christian life, and they must be embraced and applied regularly and consistently. They are not simply suggestions of how life *might* be done. They are part of an effective Christian walk. What are these instructions that are so important?

The first instruction is that Christians must present their bodies as living sacrifices to God as an act of worship. The idea of the *body* in the English language, however, can cause us to miss the point of Paul's teaching. For English speakers, the body is typically viewed as strictly the physical form that we have—our flesh, bones, and organs. However, the word translated here as body encompasses the totality of our being—both our corporeal and incorporeal forms.[2] That this is so comes not only from the Greek definition of the word translated here as body but also from the context of the passage as well. This is apparent because Paul saw the natural result of this being the transformation we will experience as our minds—which are incorporeal—are renewed. This process of renewal will result in the Christian's increased ability to no longer be shaped by the patterns of the world but shaped and influenced by the will of God. How is this accomplished?

The direct implication of the passage is this will be accomplished by the training of our powers of discernment, which will help us to identify and understand the will of God in the given situations we face. Warren Wiersbe rightly argued this ability to discern God's will comes via the Christian's personal surrender to a life of prayer and obedience.[3] Reading the scriptures is not enough. One must prayerfully consider how the word of God relates to the present circumstances in which one finds oneself and then apply the scriptural principles to life in practical ways. An example of how this might look illustrates the point.

Craig's Story

Craig is a Christian man I was working with in my executive coaching practice as he was seeking to make a career change. Rather quickly into the process, we both agreed to allow our mutual faith in Christ to shape the coaching process into the DSC we are learning about here. As Craig continued through the process of searching for a new position, he was given many opportunities to meet with leaders from various companies. Before we would meet to speak about how to approach these conversations, I would spend time praying for Craig and me to be able to hear God's voice in the situation. One day in particular, we were talking about how a certain leader Craig had been speaking with seemed to be taking longer than normal to decide if Craig was a good fit for the company. Through the use of some personality assessment material, it was becoming apparent the leader in question was not dragging his feet. Instead, he was a careful deliberator on any decision: he typically only acted when he had gained significant certainty the plan of action was the proper one. Craig, on the other hand, is the type of leader who acts more quickly and then adjusts the plan as needed to make things work.

As we talked about Craig's frustration with how slow the process was moving, God brought to mind Romans 15:1–3.

In this passage, Paul reminded Christians that it is the more mature brother or sister's responsibility to bear with the weaker brother, allowing the weaker brother or sister to set the pace and tone of the relationship. As this came to mind, I was curious as to how this applied to Craig and his situation. First, neither of us knew if Craig's potential boss was a Christian, therefore *brother* may be a misnomer. Second, and more importantly, to assume this leader was weaker than Craig simply because he was wired differently was a bit of a stretch. However, I could not shake the feeling that the principle of this scripture applied to Craig's situation.

As I continued to listen attentively to Craig, I asked God to give me insight and discernment into how this passage applied. At this point, some of the training I had in personality assessments came to mind, and I recalled that the best leaders would often intentionally modify their behavior to match the preferences of those they were dealing with. In this moment, I realized God wanted me to ask Craig how he could adjust his pace and preferences to match the pace and preferences of the company owner. As Craig considered this question, I also asked him to consider how Romans 15:1–3 might apply.

In the end, and through careful prayer and thought, Craig came to the same conclusion that I had—God wanted him to be the one to make the adjustments. Had it not been for my prayer—and Craig's prayer—both of us might have missed what God was doing. Because we were able to slow down and present our whole bodies (including our minds) to God through prayer, we discerned together the will of God in the situation. The difficulty is that not every person we are coaching and discipling is prepared for such a thing. How, then, can a discipling coach effectively bring prayer into the relationship? Let's explore this question.

PRAYER, DISCERNMENT, AND SUBMISSION TO GOD

One of the issues with DSC involving extensive prayer is the fact prayer is a spiritual discipline. By their very nature, spiritual disciplines take time and effort to develop. According to Charles Killian, this is more difficult for some people than others because the ability to develop a spiritual discipline such as prayer directly contrasts with the person's basic wiring from God. Structure and discipline come naturally to some people, while it is foreign to others.[4] From my experience over the years helping people with spiritual formation, I see that this is true. Some folks gravitate toward structured and disciplined routines to help themselves and others grow, while others deeply struggle in this area. I am one who deeply struggles; however, the struggle has been worth it.

As a Christian leader, I have been regularly exposed to the power and efficacy of prayer through the countless testimonies I have heard regarding the results. People who were infertile have become pregnant and started families, people who were on the verge of losing everything suddenly saw their fortunes turn, and incredibly difficult situations have been worked out time and again for God's glory. These answers to prayer I have witnessed and heard about have sparked within me a deep desire to see God's hand move in every area of my life, and this includes God moving in the lives of those I am discipling and coaching. I have learned, and continue to learn, to develop the discipline of prayer in my life for the benefit of others, me, and ultimately God's own glory. This relates to you, as a discipling coach, in a profound way.

Two different but related passages of scripture highlight why this is the case. The first comes from the apostle Paul and what he wrote to the church at Philippi:

And it is my prayer that your love may abound more and more, with knowledge and all discernment, so that you may approve what is excellent, and so be pure and blameless for the day of Christ, filled with the fruit of righteousness that comes through Jesus Christ, to the glory and praise of God. (Phil. 1:9–11)

This simple statement of fact that Paul is praying for the people who make up this church is a powerful reminder of the discipling coach's responsibility to engage in prayer for people—even if they are not engaged in the discipline themselves. The reason is even more profound.

Paul's purpose for praying for them is so love, knowledge, and discernment will come to them so they can know and understand the will of God. Do not miss this important point. Paul, who instructed the church at Rome to present their whole being to God in order to train the powers of discernment, explicitly stated that his prayers for another is a starting point for this very thing. N. T. Wright opined Paul gained added confidence in and for people when he constantly prayed for them as they partnered together.[5] This confidence came from his deep and abiding faith that God would be working in the lives of others as a response to Paul's disciplined prayers for them.

The reason this motivates me to pray is not merely because prayer is effective. It is also based on my understanding that my responsibility as a Christian leader, discipler, and coach is to serve others' needs above my own. This principle is embodied in the words of Jesus to his disciples as modeled for them what servant leadership looks like:

But Jesus called them to him and said, "You know that the rulers of the Gentiles lord it over them, and their great ones exercise authority over them. It shall not be so among you. But whoever would be great among you must be your servant, and whoever would be first among you must be your slave, even as the Son of Man came not to be served but to serve, and to give his life as a ransom for many." (Matt. 20:25–28)

For the Christian, we must be attentive to the needs of others, nurture them, empathize with them, put them first, and empower them to develop their full personal capacities. This is the heart of servant leadership.[6] Interestingly enough, Gary Collins made a powerful argument about coaching, especially Christian coaching: coaching is a form of servant leadership involving encouraging and challenging people to reach their full potential,[7] and this helps demonstrate how important it is to adequately apply servant leadership principles to a DSC model. How is praying, as the coach, serving others?

Besides the obvious Christian answer that prayer demonstrates our dependency on God,[8] my own story helps demonstrate this. For me, even as a pastor, praying for others is hard and easily falls by the wayside. This is because it takes time and effort on my part, and sometimes the investment does not show immediate returns. Sometimes I pray for individuals for months or even years before I see a breakthrough in their life. At other times, I pray for them and let them know I am, and it makes the relationship awkward with them. Surprisingly, on occasion, it even offends the person I am praying for. Take the stories of Shelly and Eli, for example.

Shelly's and Eli's Stories

Shelly was an executive coaching client I was serving as she worked through a career transition from one company to another. During the months we worked together, I came to admire her as a leader, even though she did not have a Christian worldview. I often searched for ways to intentionally insert kingdom principles into our conversations as a way of crossing the secular–sacred divide, but I was having very little success. As time progressed, Shelly landed a lucrative position with a new company. I knew our coaching would likely draw to a close. In a last-ditch effort, I asked Shelly if she would let me pray with her a prayer of thanksgiving for the new role. The silence on the other end of the phone was deafening. Finally, she told me she did not feel comfortable with prayer. We awkwardly moved on.

Later the same day, I sent a text to Shelly apologizing for making her feel uncomfortable with my request to pray for her. I asked for her forgiveness. Shelly replied to me rather quickly that I was forgiven. She explained the reason she felt uncomfortable with me praying for her is that her "soul was too black." In my attempt to serve her, I had caused her to come face to face with her own sinfulness in God's eyes. Shelly and I still talk from time to time, but the relationship has a different tone. To my knowledge, she is no closer to the kingdom than she was when we started, and a year later I feel as though I am fighting a battle for her with no end in sight. It is not only awkward now—it is also discouraging knowing this could go on for the rest of my life with me never seeing any positive results this side of heaven.

Eli, on the other hand, is a believer, which means what I share may make you scratch your head in dismay. As an open follower of Jesus, Eli allowed me to weave Christian principles into our coaching conversations via the DSC model. At the conclusion of each of our meetings, I let him know I was praying for him. At the end of about a year, our coaching relationship seemed to draw to a natural close. Eli had settled into some new routines and habits designed to help him reach his goals. All appeared to be well. However, after a few months of not meeting together, he contacted me, asking for a 100%

refund of the fees he had paid for coaching (he was a paying coaching client). As it turned out, the main motivator he shared for asking for a refund was that I had prayed for him. In his mind, this was offensive, although he had never told me this before, and he believed it was a way to cover up the fact I could not actually help him. I was shocked.

As I talked with Eli about this, he confessed to me that, even though he was a Christian, he viewed prayer as a pie-in-the-sky type of coping mechanism other Christians employed when they could not do things on their own. My dependency on prayer demonstrated to him I was too weak and ineffective to be of any practical assistance to him. To this day, he is still offended about the prayer. Through this, I have learned an important lesson. In some DSC relationships, ones that seek to cross the secular–sacred divide, I am going to be the only one praying. While it would seem the coachee or disciple's lack of prayer would give me permission to not pray, the opposite is actually true. Because I want the person I am helping to be able to discern God's will, I pray all the more. This is servant leadership because it is hard, takes time, and bears unexpected fruit at times. As a discipling coach, I submit myself and the person I am working with to God. Sometimes this is done mutually, as with Craig. Sometimes I am the only one participating, as with Shelly and Eli. Why even engage when the other person is not interested?

FURTHER PURPOSES OF PRAYER IN DISCIPLESHIP STYLE COACHING

While developing our powers of discernment is an important area for both the discipling coach and the coachee, there are many more things prayer does to help the process. According to E. M. Bounds, "Prayer governs conduct, and conduct makes character."[9] This is highly important because coaching, especially DSC, involves assisting people in developing new mindsets and implementing plans to pursue the best course of action in any given situation. Coaching others is largely about performance-based implementation flowing forth from increased internal development.[10] Where DSC differs from other models is in the belief this internal development is best accomplished with the guidance of God's Holy Spirit.

Building on the text of John 3:27, noted Christian thinker and pastor A. W. Tozer remarked humans are *without* the innate ability to apprehend the divine. He further explained this ability cannot be gained through Bible study, counseling with other Christians, or any other means except that which God designed. God's means was and is the indwelling Holy Spirit, who is invited into the life of a person through prayer and surrender.[11] Only when a person has surrendered to the Holy Spirit through prayer can he or she begin to receive increasing levels of guidance. This is not because God is unable. Rather, it stems from God's character and unwillingness to force a person to follow him. Thus, if discipling coaches wish to develop the character and conduct needed for effective Christian coaching, discipleship, and spiritual formation, they must surrender to and invite in the Holy Spirit of God. This begs the questions: What if the coachee or disciple is unwilling to participate? Is it still a worthwhile and effective practice?

The short answer is, *yes*! This is because the discipling coach is *not* responsible for the coachee's character and conduct. Instead, the coachee is responsible for his or her own and is also responsible for helping lay a foundation to help the coachee move in the right direction. D. Anderson and M. Anderson argued,

There is a common underlying structure of personal development that creates the foundation for lasting change and is present in all coaching relationships. The coaches who were most effective understood this dynamic and consistently laid the foundation for their clients' continued growth.[12]

As Christian discipling coaches, we are aware this foundation is best built on the unchanging truths of God as revealed by him via his Holy Spirit as we apply scriptural principles to the situations we face. The discipling coach begins to lay the foundation. He or she then fervently prays the coachee will build upon it.

Another area where prayer helps the discipling coach to develop is by increasing his or her empathetic response to those he or she is helping. "Empathy . . . [should be understood as] an imaginative act, an engagement of the compassionate imagination, an event of the understanding."[13] Empathy is closely linked to understanding, and understanding is gained through active and compassionate listening.[14] While it is possible to develop the ability to empathize without the help of God, this is best and most easily developed when the discipling coach engages in intentional prayer for—and with, when possible—the coachee.[15] Prayer opens us to the divine resources of God,[16] not the least of which is God's ability to empathize with his creations.[17]

Another specific divine resource prayer opens us to, and those we are helping, is divine peace and a lessening of worry. The reality of this is based on a divine truth Paul conveyed to Christians in Philippians 4:6–7:

Do not be anxious about anything, but in everything by prayer and supplication with thanksgiving let your requests be made known to God. And the peace of God, which surpasses all understanding, will guard your hearts and your minds in Christ Jesus.

Charles Spurgeon asserted one of the greatest truths of this passage is prayer, and the joy of the Lord as a result, is one of the best preparations Christians can make for the trials of this life.[18] My experience has shown this to be absolutely true.

Not only is it true in my life, it is true in the lives of those I have had the privilege of employing DSC coaching with. For instance, Larry recently found himself facing a set of interrelated circumstances most people would worry about. One of the major ministry teams in the church he leads went from having a full complement of workers to dissolving into nothing in less than a week. This team is one of the most visible in the church, as it is the team that leads worship music for the Sunday morning services. As Larry and I talked about this, he confessed to me how much peace and lack of worry he had about it. He wondered aloud whether or not he was being naïve. I was able to help him see this was not the case. Instead, because of his prayer and that of others, he had peace in the substantial challenge he was facing. How might this discipling moment have gone different if prayer had not been involved? Likely, it would have resulted in scrambling and brainstorming possible solutions; however, it was not this way at all. Instead, several ideas for moving forward flowed naturally into conversation, and now Larry has a plan to move forward exploring options.

Although more areas where prayer for and with those a discipling coach is helping are likely and can be discussed, one final area is explored. This area is so important to the art of coaching because it is a fundamental tenet of coaching. This area is described in the International Coach Federation's core competencies under Section 4, Coaching Presence. For a coach, even and perhaps especially a discipling coach, it is important the coach be open to not knowing and still being willing to take a risk with the coaching client.[19] As people who desire to help our fellow men and women, we are tempted to believe we must provide answers for the challenges they face. Otherwise, what good are we to them? However, as previously discussed, it is not the discipling coach's primary responsibility to provide answers. Instead, a coaching leader's primary focus should be on helping others in the process of making sense as the person being coached or discipled finds his or her own answers.[20]

Prayer declares our dependence on God by admitting we have no worthwhile answers apart from him. This is similar to the lyrics of the song *I Know a Man Who Can*.[21] In this song, the writer conveyed his inability to heal, restore, perform miracles, or do anything of worth for other people, declaring instead he knew a man who could. The man he knew was and *is* the embodiment of God—Jesus Christ. R. Kent Hughes argued of this type of dependency, if Jesus, while he walked the earth, could not function without this type of dependency, what makes any of us believe we can or should?[22] In our dependency on God via prayer we affirm as DSC practitioners we are comfortable with not knowing all the answers and still helping people move forward. This comfort level is not fabricated. It comes via the indwelling of the Holy Spirit as we submit all things to God in prayer.

Larry's Story and His Calling to Ministry

In 2007, Larry had been attending the church I was leading and planting for about four years, and he had attended the mother church of the plant for an additional two years. During those six years, he had grown by leaps and bounds and was serving in a volunteer capacity in many areas. However, he consistently had a deep and pervading sense God was calling him to much more. This sense of calling was especially prevalent in his life at the yearly mission conferences the church held. These conferences are short festivals and teaching times where we bring in international Christian workers to share about their ministry in foreign lands, as well as challenge the people of the local church to serve with a missionary heart. For years, Larry would be at the altar at the conclusion of these conferences promising God he would do more for the kingdom. But the new actions attached to the promise rarely lasted long before he would return to his regular ministry habits. However, because of prayer and DSC, 2007 would see Larry take a different path.

I can vividly remember asking Larry what it would look like if he placed the proverbial stake in the ground at the conclusion of mission conference and went forward with what he sensed God's plan for his life was. Through a time of joint prayer, Larry offered himself to the Lord as a living sacrifice and began the discernment process of what moving forward would look like. In a response to Larry's prayer, the Holy Spirit filled him anew and began guiding him as he developed a plan to move forward. Part of this involved the Holy Spirit revealing areas where Larry's character and conduct needed some alterations. As we engaged in DSC, Larry developed goals and accountability plans to develop the character he needed and change his conduct. A large portion of this involved the discipline needed to further his education.

Before long, Larry was enrolled in an undergraduate degree program to get the needed education for vocational ministry. Much of this was a struggle for Larry, but the Lord helped me to have empathy for him in the process, empathy Larry credited as being instrumental to helping him move forward. All the while, I did not have many answers for Larry;

however, as we both declared our dependence on God, the answers eventually came. What is more, many of the answers should have caused worry in Larry from a worldly point of view. For instance, how would he pay for college? How would he balance his work, a full course load, and his volunteer activities during this period, or even how would his family cope? However, God continued to give him peace, and Larry achieved both an undergraduate and a master's degree by the time he was done with all his schooling. All the while, God used prayer to empower the process.

As of this writing, Larry is serving as the lead pastor in the church where the story started. The ministry has flourished under his leadership, and other Christ followers have been engaged in the DSC process with similar results. Larry's story serves as a constant reminder of how prayer is extensively involved if the DSC model is to be effective in helping people cross the secular–sacred divide.

---

1 Thomas, R. L. (1998). *New American standard Hebrew-Aramaic and Greek dictionaries: Updated edition.* Anaheim, CA: Foundation Publications, Inc.

2 Calvin, J., & Owen, J. (2010). *Commentary on the epistle of Paul the apostle to the romans.* Bellingham, WA: Logos Bible Software, p. 452.

3 Wiersbe, W. W. (1992). *Wiersbe's expository outlines on the new testament.* Wheaton, IL: Victor Books, p. 399.

4 Killian, C. (1996). Disciplines for the undisciplined. In M. Shelley (Ed.), *Deepening your ministry through prayer and personal growth: 30 strategies to transform your ministry.* Nashville, TN: Moorings.

5 Wright, N. T. (2004). *Paul for everyone: The prison letters: Ephesians, Philippians, Colossians, and Philemon.* London, England: Society for Promoting Christian Knowledge, p. 85.

6 Northouse, P. G. (2013). *Leadership: Theory and practice* (6th ed.). Thousand Oaks, CA: Sage, p. 219.

7 Collins, G. R. (2002). Christian coaching: *Helping others turn potential into reality* (2nd ed.). Colorado Springs, CO: Navpress, p. 41.

8 Water, M. (1998). *Knowing God's will made easier.* Carlisle, UK: Hunt & Thorpe, p. 18.

9 Bounds, E. M. (1990). *The complete works of E. M. Bounds on prayer.* Grand Rapids, MI: Baker Books, p. 47.

10 Hagen, M. S., Bialek, T. K., & Peterson, S. L. (2017). The nature of peer coaching: Definitions, goals, processes, and outcomes. *European Journal of Training and Development, 41*(6), 540–558.

11 Tozer, A. W. (2009). *The counselor: Straight talk about the holy spirit.* Camp Hill, PA: Wing Spread Publishers, pp. 18–34.

12 Anderson, D., & Anderson, M. (2011). *Coaching that counts: Harnessing the power of leadership coaching to deliver strategic value.* New York, NY: Routledge, p. 6.

13 Oden, T. C. (1989). *Pastoral counsel.* New York, NY: Crossroad, p. 9.

14 Passmore, J., & Oades, L. G. (2014). Positive psychology techniques—Active constructive responding. *Coaching Psychologist, 10*(2), 71–73.

15 Rees, P. S. (1974). Prayer and social concern. *Reformed Journal, 24*(1), 8–11.

16 Bounds, 1990, p. 350.

17 Oden, 1989, p. 9.

18 Spurgeon, C. (2014). *Spurgeon commentary: Philippians* (E. Ritzema, Ed.). Bellingham, WA: Lexham Press, p. 143.

19 See https://coachfederation.org/core-competencies for the core competencies set out by the International Coach Federation.

20 Angélique, D. T. (2007). Making sense through coaching. *The Journal of Management Development, 26*(3), 282–291.

2 *I Know a Man Who Can* is a Christian song written by Jack Campbell and Jimmie Davis and released by singer George Jones.

22 Hughes, R. K. (1998). *Luke: That you may know the truth.* Wheaton, IL: Crossway Books, p. 207.

CHAPTER 6

Developing Effective Listening and Questioning Skills

And Peter answered him, "Lord, if it is you, command me to come to you on the water." He said, "Come." So Peter got out of the boat and walked on the water and came to Jesus. But when he saw the wind, he was afraid, and beginning to sink he cried out, "Lord, save me." Jesus immediately reached out his hand and took hold of him, saying to him, "O you of little faith, why did you doubt?" And when they got into the boat, the wind ceased. And those in the boat worshiped him, saying, "Truly you are the Son of God." (Matt. 14:28–33)

One of the major tenets for coaching, even the discipleship style coaching (DSC) model, is the need for those engaging in the practices and principles to train their abilities to listen effectively and ask appropriate and powerful questions. For those of us who engage in DSC, this goes beyond the International Coach Federation's core competency of communicating effectively by actively listening to the coachee.[1] Effective Christian listening has one ear tuned to the person one is helping and one ear tuned to what the Holy Spirit is speaking into the situation.[2] With such active listening, discipling coaches develop the discernment to ask powerful questions that challenge assumptions and help others develop plans to move forward effectively in the situations they face. The disciples' encounter with Jesus as he walked on the water highlights how this works.

THE PASSAGE EXPLORED

Before digging into the pericope in question, it is important to note how Matthew recorded in 14:22–23 Jesus instructing the disciples to go over to the other side of the lake while he went up on the mountain alone to pray. There are two reasons for this. The first reason is it helps us understand why Jesus was not in the boat with the disciples in the first place. The second reason is subtler, and it is the more important of the two. As discussed in the previous chapter, the DSC model involves extensive prayer, and this is what Jesus modeled here. Before this encounter with the disciples, Jesus spent an extended time in prayer. This time of prayer helped prepare him for the encounter on the water as he heard the voice of the Father via the Holy Spirit guiding him in his interactions with the disciples.[3] Without this time of prayer and dependence on God, would Jesus have been able to engage Peter and the others in this way? I believe the answer is both yes and no. *Yes*, because Jesus is God made manifest in the flesh (John 1:14), thus he had continual access to the divine attributes of God via his intimate connection with him. *No*, because Jesus had laid aside his divinity in order to model for us what it looked like to operate in a Spirit-empowered way (Phil. 2:5–7). In light of this, we approach the passage from the lens of the answer being no.

After Jesus' time of prayer, he had to catch up with his disciples. As those men had left the place where Jesus was to cross over to the other side, they encountered an intense storm that hampered their progress as they attempted to head toward their goal. Because of this, the disciples experiencing heightened anxiety. So when they saw Jesus approaching them on the water, they cried out in terror, believing they were seeing some sort of apparition. However, Jesus called out to them in an effort to calm them and let them know that it was he who was approaching their boat (Matt. 14:24–27).

Upon hearing it was Jesus approaching them, Peter came up with the most interesting response. Instead of sitting in total amazement, he told Jesus if it was really him, then he should tell Peter to come to him on the water. Jesus' time of prayer had prepared him to listen to Peter in a way that brought about remarkable results. Rather than saying, "No, you wait there for me," Jesus obliged him by instructing him to get out of the boat and come to him. N. T. Wright posited this response from Jesus came from his understanding that even the most faithful of disciples usually operated somewhere on the sliding scale between total doubt and disbelief to full and total confidence. Jesus knew there was something deeper behind Peter's request than to simply walk on the water. This was an important moment for Peter and the other disciples as they were learning how to live out kingdom principles in their lives.[4]

What happened next is informative for discipling coaches who are striving to help others. Peter, as he walked on the water, achieved mixed results. For a few moments, he had great success. However, as he saw and heard the storm raging, he began to fail and sink. These mixed results bear a striking similarity to the patterns I have witnessed with those I have employed the DSC model with. This pattern of success and failure is not one to be avoided. It is an expected part of the process as people attempt to employ new practices designed to help them move forward in their business and personal lives and cross the secular–sacred divide.[5]

Jesus' response to Peter as he began to fail demonstrates for us how listening is done with both the physical eyes and ears, as well as inner ears tuned to what God is saying in the situation. Without this perspective, we are tempted to look at Jesus' response to Peter as a simple rebuke for lacking faith. However, this lens reveals something happening on a deeper level. Jesus was not rebuking Peter. He was asking Peter to learn from his situation—why his doubt caused him to sink. Ponder this observation for a moment.

Jesus, as the ultimate example of a discipling coach, observed through all of his senses—including his extended time of prayer—that Peter was at a crossroads of learning. Rather than providing Peter with a trite bit of advice on how to overcome the obstacles standing in his way, Jesus asked him a powerful question intended to help Peter wrestle with his own success and failures. Akin to the International Coach Federation core competencies, Jesus did not provide answers to his disciple. Instead, he helped Peter reframe his current reality, taking stock of his strengths and weaknesses and the opportunities and threats he was facing. This bit of active listening and questioning evoked a most unexpected response from all the disciples. They concluded Jesus is truly God in the flesh, and they worshipped him.

One major lesson we can learn from this is Jesus, by his use of active listening and questioning, helped the disciples arrive in the place they each needed to without him giving any advice or clear-cut guidance. Instead, Jesus trusted each of his disciples were generally healthy when it came to emotional and spiritual health. In fact, they were already successful men in their respective trades or professions. This core belief in their general health allowed Jesus to trust in the process I describe here. It ultimately served as a major catalyst in helping this group of men become the exceptional leaders who would launch the worldwide movement of Christianity we see today.

One particular DSC relationship stands out as a good example of this type of active listening and questioning—the story of Raylene.

Raylene's Story

Raylene was a paying coaching client of mine for about eight months. She had recently quit her job at a large medical software company because they were asking her to overlook glitches in the program that would allow medical providers in different locations to prescribe medicines to patients . . . with deadly interactions. As an ethical and Christian software quality analyst, Raylene could not abide the company's course of action. She left the company and sought my help in pursuing a new role.

Rather quickly into our times together, Raylene divulged she was a Christian. In light of this revelation, I sought permission from her to openly integrate kingdom principles into our meetings. She agreed. As we worked together, Raylene would have both good and bad moments. Sometimes she second-guessed her decision to leave the company she had been working for without having something else lined up, but the past was in the past. All she could do was work on a plan to move forward. As I prayed for Raylene, I could not help but empathize with her discouragement in the job search. Besides needing money to pay bills, she was beginning to feel worthless without something to work on. This is when I used a powerful question: "Is there some way you can use your talents on something other than a job?" She pondered this question and concluded she should volunteer at her local church helping others. For several weeks, this helped her maintain focus, and then she landed a new role with another company.

It was exciting for Raylene to embark upon a new journey. However, as the disciples experienced, the wind and waves did not cease. On the first day of her new role, Raylene was let go because the company lost a major contract. Even though her new boss let her know she was not at fault, Raylene was crushed. In one moment, she was walking on water. In the next moment, she began to sink. Inevitably, Raylene spiraled into more doubt. I asked her a series of questions to begin moving forward again.

One of those questions was, "What skills or abilities do you need to acquire for the types of roles you are looking for?" She decided there was a relevant course in project management and another in software quality assurance automation she should enroll in. While going to school to gain these skills, Raylene and I kept in contact monthly with coaching sessions, and she continued to volunteer at her church to keep herself busy while helping others. While in school, Raylene applied for various roles she thought she fit, but it seemed no company was interested in her. Via a time of prayer, the Lord prompted me to ask her another powerful question: "Have you ever considered a business analyst role with a software development firm? This question rocked Raylene's world as it opened her to a new realm of possibilities.

As Raylene researched these types of roles, she found she was highly qualified to do this work. She began pursuing these roles while also looking for quality assurance positions. After a long and arduous search, Raylene accepted a role with a new company she was extremely excited about. Even more amazing than this, Raylene actually received five job offers in the same week she accepted this new position. She went from feeling desperate to realizing she could add tremendous value to multiple companies.

Importantly, Raylene accepted the job that was not the highest paying of the offers. She chose to go with the company where she felt she could make the biggest impact for the king-dom of God as she put her skills to use in the business world. I shudder to think what would have happened if I had not listened to Raylene and asked powerful questions and instead had proceeded to give her my advice. She might still be unem-ployed or worse—employed in the wrong company!

DEVELOPING ACTIVE LISTENING SKILLS

Developing active listening skills is not easy, but it is possible even for the most seasoned advice givers and talkers. I should know because my years as a pastor and leader have condi-tioned me to provide advice and answers to people who are struggling to find them. However, coaching in general, and DSC coaching specifically, have served as the catalyst for me to develop the active listening skills needed to provide lead-ership-affirming and life-changing assistance to those I have had the pleasure of coming alongside over the years. The pri-mary way active listening can affirm leadership is when it is integrated into a solid coaching mentality. It greatly enhances the leadership self-efficacy of those we help. People become more confident in their own leadership abilities. Some studies have indicated this confidence goes up by as much as 27%.[7] People are affirmed in their abilities to lead themselves and others. This is life changing because it helps them function better in complex and dynamic environments. What, then, are the practical skills that make up this critical skill set?

Jonathan Passmore and Alison Whybrow argued there are two skills coaching practitioners should develop to hone the craft of active listening: (a) making reflective listening statements and (b) offering affirmations. The essence of reflective listening is the coach checking the meaning of what the coachee has said, rather than assuming what was meant. And offering affirmations facilitates an atmosphere of acceptance, which helps build confidence in the hearts and minds of coachees and disciples.[8] So let's explore reflective listening statements.

Jesus used reflective listening statements on numerous occasions. One such example is recorded in Luke 24:17–19a while Jesus was walking along with two of his followers on the Emmaus road before they knew he had been resurrected:

> *And he said to them, "What is this conversation that you are holding with each other as you walk?" And they stood still, looking sad. Then one of them, named Cleopas, answered him, "Are you the only visitor to Jerusalem who does not know the things that have happened there in these days?" And he said to them, "What things?"*

This example of reflective listening is so powerful. If anyone could safely assume what someone else meant by their statements it would have been Jesus. However, instead of assuming, Jesus asked a simple, but powerful, question meant to help his followers clarify in their own minds and hearts the issues they were dealing with.

M. S. Mills posited the reason Jesus did this is significant because it demonstrates compassion and empathy for two lowly disciples as they walked a dusty road with downtrodden hearts.[9] He could have simply told them who he was, cheered them up, and then sent them back on their mission. Instead,

Jesus' practical concern and availability to others as he utilized reflective listening, meant to bring out the deeper meanings of what was being said, shows us how transformative reflective listening statements and powerful questions can be as evidenced by their reaction once they knew the truth of his resurrection. Even though the day had worn away, "They rose that same hour and returned to Jerusalem. And they found the eleven and those who were with them gathered together" (Luke 24:33).

Jesus is well known for offering affirmations as well. While this happened with those who were already disciples of his, it often happened with those who were not yet part of the kingdom. One such example comes from the story of the Canaanite woman whose daughter was suffering from demon possession:

> *And Jesus went away from there and withdrew to the district of Tyre and Sidon. And behold, a Canaanite woman from that region came out and was crying, "Have mercy on me, O Lord, Son of David; my daughter is severely oppressed by a demon." But he did not answer her a word. And his disciples came and begged him, saying, "Send her away, for she is crying out after us." He answered, "I was sent only to the lost sheep of the house of Israel." But she came and knelt before him, saying, "Lord, help me." And he answered, "It is not right to take the children's bread and throw it to the dogs." She said, "Yes, Lord, yet even the dogs eat the crumbs that fall from their masters' table." Then Jesus answered her, "O woman, great is your faith! Be it done for you as you desire." And her daughter was healed instantly." (Matt. 15:21–28)*

A reason this is such a great example of Jesus offering affirmations is because he waited until his disciples were present to respond to the woman in question. Jesus could have easily had this exchange in private with the woman, but he chose to wait until his disciples were present to respond to her. At first, his response did not seem too affirming. In essence, he told the woman, "Look, I came for the people of Israel, and it would not be right for me to give to you what is rightfully theirs." For some, this may have been demoralizing, but not for this desperate mother. His initial response was reflective, though not a question, designed to draw out of her what she was really after. When she responded that even a scrap of his power was enough, he was pleased to help her by setting her daughter free. In the process, he affirmed her faith in him, which was instrumental in setting her on a course of further trust in him. I used these two active listening techniques—reflective listening statements and offering affirmations—to great effect in many of my DSC relationships. One such example is in the story of Chrissy.

Chrissy's Story

One of the most powerful and informative issues in Chrissy's story is that a great deal of reflective listening and affirmation offering were *not* involved in the beginning. The main reason behind this is because Chrissy reported to me in one of the churches I served in as she oversaw the adult discipleship ministries of the church. As such, I interacted with her more often as a supervisor than as a discipling coach, providing direction and guidance for her as she sought to implement sound discipleship principles. However, one day she said something that rocked me to my core. During a coaching session, she told me others were providing negative feedback to her about the things she was trying to implement. The most common feedback she was receiving was everything she was doing was the things I was making her do, and people wanted her to lead on her own without so much direct influence from me. While I never directly told Chrissy this, I realized on that day I had not been coaching her with the DSC method I describe here. I had been using her as my proxy to implement my own agenda for adult ministries. Things were about to change.

Even before I began serving at this particular church, they had been using a costly online Bible study curriculum as they attempted to make disciples who made disciples. One of the primary issues I had been charged with upon accepting my assignment to this church was implementing cost controls to bring the unwieldy and growing budget under control before it bankrupted the church. In my mind, this online curriculum was one major cost the church should cut. I worked on how to remove the recurring fees associated with its use. This caused me to react to Chrissy with a command-and-control style of leadership that was hidden behind the guise of DSC. However, it was not affirming Chrissy as a leader, and it was certainly not changing her life for the better.

As a result of this revelation, I decided to intentionally implement reflective listening skills and offer regular affirmations when I could. During our next session, Chrissy shared some of the challenges she had gaining and training new teachers. Rather than assuming I knew what she meant, I asked her why she thought this was the case. She brought up several problem areas in curriculum delivery, including unstable internet and the lack of good projection equipment. Chrissy was convinced she could make this material work if she simply had the technology she needed. I asked her who she could utilize in the church to stabilize the internet and what she felt she would need for equipment. I had assumed she would want to buy a lot of new equipment, but I did not tell her this—probing instead with reflective listening statements and questions. To my surprise, she had developed a brilliant plan to repurpose several pieces of projection equipment. I quickly offered affirmation.

This day of *actual* DSC changed the tone of our relationship. Chrissy took more control of her own ministry responsibilities because of it. While there were still occasions where I fell back into my old habits, I was largely able to turn this DSC relationship to a much more positive set of experiences as I applied the two active listening techniques. Active listening and powerful questioning, however, does not end with these two skills.

OTHER ACTIVE LISTENING SKILLS AND TECHNIQUES

Tom Lewis and Gerald Graham provided multiple strategies to develop active listening.[10] The first strategy is cultivating the ability to concentrate on what others are saying. While this may seem obvious, it is more difficult than one might expect. This is largely because people are able to process faster than people typically speak, sometimes as much as five times faster. It is critical for discipling coaches to diligently remove outside distractions—turn off phones, meet in a private location where it is quiet, eliminate interruptions during the meeting, turn off email alerts (especially if the coach is using a computer to take notes), and intentionally refocus on the conversation if and when thoughts begin to drift. Closely related to the above is sending the speaker both verbal and nonverbal cues of listening—nodding agreement while the speaker is talking, physically leaning forward, making appropriate eye contact, and the avoidance of playing with things with one's hands.

Another skill that greatly enhances active listening is the ability to effectively paraphrase what the other person is saying. Paraphrasing is both a skill and art where the person listening repeats to the speaker the message they received in their own words.[11] Active listening is more of an organic process, rather than mechanical. Solid paraphrasing has been shown to greatly enhance this, building trust with the speaker as the discipling coach demonstrates understanding by accurately paraphrasing what the other is saying.[12] Paraphrasing also helps in clarification because it potentially exposes any misunderstanding about what has been communicated. I have found when I paraphrase what others are saying I receive one of two responses: (a) affirmation from the coachee that I have understood correctly or (b) explanation of areas I did not understand. This is critical for two reasons. The first is it may demonstrate where the coach has not been listening as well as he or she thought. The second is its ability to help coachees understand where they may not be explaining what they think, feel, or believe clearly enough for the receiver to completely grasp the meaning.

The final technique of active listening is listening and observing for feelings the speaker is sharing. Listening and observing for feelings involves actively concentrating on the body language, tone of voice, and other nonverbal cues the speaker is sending. Giving primacy to the feelings, rather than the words spoken, can greatly assist discipling coaches, as well as the coachee, in deciphering the deeper meanings present in what is being said.[13] Examples of listening and observing for feelings, and the insights provided by it, follow.

One of the most telling signs of feelings I have experienced while employing the DSC model with those with whom I work is in the area of eye contact. Countless people I have worked with over the years have had marked changes in their ability to make eye contact during different portions of a meeting. This has happened in various ways. For instance, sometimes a person has a history of making strong eye contact during sessions but then suddenly is unwilling to meet my gaze. When I notice this happening, it helps me to understand something deeper is going on. Whether or not to address this directly is a matter of intuition that a discipling coach must trust.

I was helping Tony, a Christian chief financial officer (CFO), make a career transition. For several sessions, we had been working on helping Tony develop better interviewing skills. While we practiced various questions, his eyes would never meet mine. However, when I asked him an extremely technical finance question, he looked directly at me, the tone of his voice conveyed confidence, and he engaged better than ever before. I paused the role-playing session to understand what happened. Tony explained that he felt the most confident when interview questions dealt with the technical aspects of a CFO's role. As we explored this, Tony discovered he could feel as confident with nontechnical questions if he conducted research on potential interview questions beforehand. This shaped his future interview preparations. Shortly thereafter, he started a new role. All of this came about because I noticed the feelings he conveyed via eye contact.

Another individual I was helping was great at making eye contact. However, I noticed that any time we spoke about her reaching out to begin new professional relationships, she would immediately look down and away. This clued me into the amount of discomfort she felt when being the initiator of these types of encounters, and it helped us to know we needed to design a plan where she could gain confidence in this area. In a relatively short time, she was feeling more confident in this area and able to manage her own career more effectively.

Other areas of nonverbal communication that have helped me discover coachees' feelings are their tone of voice, changes in the rate of speech, and fidgeting. When these things change, they are great indicators of something going on internally that needs to be explored. Fidgeting usually conveys nervousness about the topic at hand, whereas tone and rate changes indicate a myriad of feelings—hostility, shame, increased confidence, and so on. Reflective listening statements are instrumental in uncovering unspoken feelings. One such reflective listening statement I have found extremely effectively is "Your tone of voice [or rate of speech] noticeably changed just now. What is happening internally to cause this?" Such open-ended questions are simple but powerful questions discipling coaches should employ as they assist others in the DSC process.

With this in mind, we return to Larry's story to see how all of these active listening skills can greatly enhance a DSC engagement.

Larry's Story Revisited

Several years into the ongoing relationship with Larry, God provided the means to bring him on as a full-time staff member of the church I was planting. His new role as a paid staff member, with me as his supervisor, clouded the DSC relationship to some degree. As with Chrissy, I often found myself floundering as I worked to balance the dual roles of discipling coach and supervisor. One such instance involved Larry's purchase and use of a motorcycle.

The church-planting team was searching for creative ways to engage the community on the level of genuine friendships and shared interests. In the region of the country where the church was situated, riding motorcycles as a group was gaining popularity. This naturally led to many of the people buying bikes and starting our own riding group. Larry enthusiastically embraced this idea and purchased a motorcycle. However, for riding a motorcycle, a special endorsement is needed on your driver's license. While Larry knew he needed this endorsement, he was struggling with making the time to go and take the needed road test.

At this same time, several scandals involving pastors rocked our community. One of these involved a pastor breaking the law, which gained a lot of negative media attention. In light of this, I felt it was my responsibility as Larry's supervisor to ensure he was compliant with the law involving the safe and legal operation of a motorcycle. On several occasions, we spoke of his need to discontinue riding his motorcycle until he was legally compliant. The problem, as Larry saw it, was the busyness of ministry was interfering with his ability to go and take the test. I found switching to the role of a discipling coach was helpful.

During one of our conversations on this issue, Larry had a marked change in his tone of voice and normal mode of eye contact. As I worked to actively listen to him, his tone became defensive, and he also went from making normal eye contact to staring directly in my eyes the whole time. Rather than assuming I knew what was happening, I asked him why the sudden changes. With a bit of probing, he confessed he was angry with me for making such a big deal of this issue. In his mind, it would only involve him receiving a ticket if he was stopped for some reason. At this point, I fought back the urge to become defensive myself.

I asked Larry what he thought the likely outcome would be if he had some type of accident involving his motorcycle. He initially tried to focus on the physical damage to himself and his property, at which point I switched gears by asking him about the recent scandals in our city. At first, Larry had difficultly connecting the dots but eventually concluded that, with the current climate in our city, the newspapers would probably make a big deal about another pastor thinking he or she could operate outside of the law. He further surmised that even though this was a small item in the relative scope of things, it could easily be blown out of proportion in the local papers. I asked him what he needed to do in order to protect against this.

Larry broke off eye contact while becoming hostile in his tone of voice again. Using probing questions, I got him to share what he was feeling. In Larry's mind, he thought the joy of riding his motorcycle was going to be off the table for a long while because our busy church schedule would prevent him from getting his license. To say I was surprised is an understatement. I was Larry's supervisor, and I knew I would allow him the needed time to get his license. Yet, Larry could not see this. Rather than tell him, I asked another set of questions.

These questions involved getting him to place himself in his supervisor's shoes. I asked him to think through what his supervisor wanted and how both people's needs could be addressed. His answer was that he thought his supervisor (who was me) only cared about protecting the name of the church. He concluded I would want him to park his motorcycle until he could make time on his own to get the license. Rather than correct him, I asked how this would support the church's ministry to motorcycle riders. He rightly concluded it would not, at which point he explored other options. As we talked for several more minutes, Larry concluded I wanted him to enjoy his motorcycle as much or more than he did. When this revelation hit him, I asked him what we could do together to ensure this happened. After a bit of back and forth, Larry decided the only way forward was for me to allow him time during the work day to get his license, which I was willing to do all along. While it would have been easier in some ways to tell him this from the beginning, I knew there was value in helping him to reach this conclusion on his own. We agreed he could take time off the next day to complete the needed road test for his license, and we put in some items to keep him accountable to this plan.

While this story might seem trivial, even a waste of coaching on some level, it actually helped Larry and I develop our DSC relationship. It helped Larry to understand that as his supervisor, and more importantly his coach, I was interested in helping him to achieve his personal goals in a manner that glorified God and strengthened our interpersonal relationship. As a result, our communication with each other on every issue we encountered flowed far more effectively as trust was deepened between us. This was enabled by active listening designed to help Larry develop personally, professionally, and spiritually, rather than simply getting him to comply with my desires as the supervisor and discipling coach. Larry now uses these same techniques with his staff, church members, and others as he engages in DSC.

---

1 See https://coachfederation.org/core-competencies for the core competencies set out by the International Coach Federation.

2 Christian Coaches Network International has developed a white paper on the subject of the distinctions of Christian coaching as opposed to secular coaching (see https://christiancoaches.com/wp-content/uploads/2017/10/CCNI-Christian-Coaching-Distinctions.pdf). One of the primary distinctions is the reliance on the Holy Spirit as an active participant in the coaching process.

3 Rosscup, J. E. (2008). *An exposition on prayer in the Bible: Igniting the fuel to flame our communication with God.* Bellingham, WA: Lexham Press, p. 1543.

4 Wright, N. T. (2004). *Matthew for everyone, part 1: Chapters 1–15.* London, England: Society for Promoting Christian Knowledge, p. 189.

5 Brantley, M. E. (2007). *Executive coaching and deep learning* (Order No. 3255517). Available from ABI/INFORM Collection. The author relates multiple case studies where the success and failures of a normal learning cycle were part and parcel to coachees moving forward into an area of increasingly better results. What is interesting about this study is Brantley utilized many of the DSC model techniques outlined herein, although he did not refer to it in this manner.

6 In software development companies, a business analyst is someone who helps gather user requirements for software and then translates those requirements into usable information for coders and programmers as they design software updates and upgrades.

7 Grant, A. M., Studholme, I., Verma, R., Kirkwood, L., Paton, B., & O'Connor, S. (2017). The impact of leadership coaching in an Australian healthcare setting. *Journal of Health Organization and Management, 31*(2), 237–252.

8 Passmore, J., & Whybrow, A. (2007). Motivational interviewing: A specific approach for coaching psychologists In S. Palmer, & A. Whybrow (Eds.), *Handbook of coaching psychology* (pp. 160–173). New York, NY: Routledge.

9 Mills, M. S. (1999). *The life of Christ: A study guide to the gospel record.* Dallas, TX: 3E Ministries.

10 Lewis, T. D., & Graham, G. (2003). 7 tips for effective listening. *The Internal Auditor, 60*(4), 23–25.

11 Lewis & Graham, 2003, p. 24.

12 Tyler, J. A. (2011). Reclaiming rare listening as a means of organizational re-enchantment. *Journal of Organizational Change Management, 24*(1), 143–157.

13 Tyler, 2011, p. 151.

CHAPTER 7

Setting the Agenda for DSC Encounters

And the eunuch said to Philip, "About whom, I ask you, does the prophet say this, about himself or about someone else?" Then Philip opened his mouth, and beginning with this Scripture he told him the good news about Jesus. And as they were going along the road they came to some water, and the eunuch said, "See, here is water! What prevents me from being baptized?" And he commanded the chariot to stop, and they both went down into the water, Philip and the eunuch, and he baptized him. (Acts 8:34–38)

One major way discipleship style coaching (DSC) differs from the more traditional models of discipleship and spiritual formation used by the church is in setting the agenda for meetings. As noted in Chapter 2, the bulk of the discipleship material available today comes with preplanned agendas as laid out in lesson plans. These types of Bible study are useful, especially in a group setting. However, the DSC model focuses on one-on-one interactions between the discipling coach and the individual seeking help, thus this type of material has more limited use—if at all. This is largely due to the free-flowing nature of DSC encounters where the coachee can explore and reflect upon the issues most pertinent to him or her in that moment. Because these are one-on-one encounters, the coachee can and should be encouraged to set a personalized agenda for the time spent with the discipling coach.

This can be uncomfortable for coaches less experienced with the DSC model because the conversation may explore areas where the coach may feel ill equipped. However, discipling coaches who have developed the discipline of prayer, active listening, and powerful questioning need not fear this because the Holy Spirit is more than capable of providing the needed skills to effectively cope with unexpected turns in the conversation. This is evident in the encounter recorded between Philip and the Ethiopian eunuch recorded in Acts 8.

THE PASSAGE EXPLORED

The verses that start this chapter are part of a larger narrative contained in Acts 8:26–40, wherein commentator Philip Bence noted how God utilized a combination of the miraculous coupled with human effort to help the Ethiopian eunuch grow in his personal faith in the God of Israel. Via his indwelling Spirit, God instructed Philip two times to approach the chariot of the Ethiopian eunuch in order to assist him in his journey of faith (Acts 8:26, 29).[1] This is important for the DSC model because it demonstrates how Philip's life of disciplined prayer played a critical role as he listened to the voice of the Holy Spirit guiding him in this encounter.[2] It is also important to note the Spirit of God did not tell Philip exactly what to do upon arriving at the eunuch's chariot. Philip engaged the skills of inquiry and active listening he had developed, which helped him to quickly understand the most pressing matter on the heart of the man he would be coaching and guiding in the process of spiritual formation.

The first thing Philip noticed was the Ethiopian was reading aloud from the book of Isaiah. Philip then asked him about his understanding of this passage. The eunuch confessed he did not really understand what he was reading and needed help from someone as he wrestled with the spiritual truths contained in the passage. Philip obliged the eunuch in this endeavor, allowing him to set the agenda for their time together. Though the content of the entire conversation is not recorded, it is evident from the outcome that Philip helped the Ethiopian eunuch to understand Jesus was the Messiah prophesied in the passage he was reading.[3] Even more telling from this encounter about who sets the agenda is the eunuch's response to Philip's help in understanding—he desired to be baptized after receiving Jesus as his Lord and Savior.

In my experience with the church's modern discipling methodologies, the Ethiopian eunuch's request to be baptized immediately would have largely fallen on deaf ears. This is because many churches have been indoctrinated into the practice of only baptizing new converts either after converts have participated in a predesigned study on the meaning and importance of baptism via an intensive study on its practice or at select times of the year. However, Philip was not constrained. He allowed this new convert to set the agenda, baptized him when they came upon water, and then was whisked away by the Spirit of God to another location. While Philip's actions may seem strange, even extreme, to modern Christians, they clearly bear the blessing of God. Many commentators and theologians even have argued this one encounter was a critical step in taking the gospel deep into Gentile territories such as Africa.[4]

My Personal Story

Years ago, I had an encounter that bore some striking similarities to the one between Peter and the Ethiopian. I was serving at a Christian summer camp during a high school retreat. During the week-long camp, the students and staff were experiencing a revival. Many of the youth present were being set free from the bondages to sin they had experienced in their lives. One young lady in particular was released from long-term demonic oppression she had been suffering from for years due to dabbling with the occult. This freedom in Christ came on the first night of the camp, and the experience was so intense it shifted the entire agenda for the week.

This happened on the morning of the second day of camp as the students and staff requested we shift the week's plans away from a typical camping experience and delve deeper into what a Spirit-filled life looked like. This request caused all of the other workers and me to restructure the week around intensive discipleship, as opposed to the regular camp fare of ropes courses, team-building events, games, and the like. For an average of five to six hours a day, the students sat attentively in meetings hastily designed to explore the myriad of questions they had about faith. This came because of the encounter we all had the first evening of camp. I wisely allowed the students to set the agenda for the week in response.

As the week continued, the camp participants grew in their faith in ways I have never experienced before or since with such a large group (although I have had this happen with individuals as I employed the DSC model). All the students, except one, present at the camp either gave their life to Christ for the first time or rededicated themselves to his service. At the end of the week, 17 of those present requested to be baptized before they went home from camp. All of the workers present agreed they heard the Spirit of God prompting them to oblige this request. It was a very wet and awesome evening filled with great joy and celebration.

In under a week's time, I was called on the carpet by these students' pastors and my denominational leaders and asked why I thought it appropriate to baptize these young people. No matter how I tried to explain, my allowing the students to set the agenda greatly offended other Christian leaders. For those not present at the camp, they could not fathom why I would break with the tradition of having their own church staff baptize the students after an intensive Bible study on the meaning and purpose of baptism.

Even though I got into trouble, I do not regret the decision I made to allow these young disciples to set the agenda for the week. Multiple full-time Christian workers eventually emerged from this week of camp, including at least one foreign missionary. I do not know if the results would have been the same had I followed the agenda set for the week. Perhaps the kingdom of God would have been advanced just as strongly. I do know, however, that by allowing those I was assisting with their spiritual formation to set the agenda, lives were dramatically and powerfully changed, and the gospel continues to spread to people far and wide as a result.

DRAWING OUT THE COACHEE'S/DISCIPLE'S AGENDA

In the above story, I *accidentally* discovered the agenda of a group of Christ followers as we explored the faith in a time set apart for that. However, I have learned over the years of employing the DSC model this can be done on purpose and with regularity. But how can this be effectively and consistently accomplished for discipling coaches working with coaches and disciples? Apply the DSC model! This involves the previously discussed areas of viewing disciples as generally healthy and capable of positive change, engaging in extensive and disciplined prayer, actively listening and responding with powerful questioning, and intentionally applying the GROW (i.e., goals, reality, opportunities/obstacles, way forward) framework as DSC practitioners seize every opportunity to coach and disciple others. There is a mindset discipling coaches can and should develop to ensure this happens.

This mindset is that the coachee or disciple knows best what he or she needs to continue to improve in every area of life. This is true whether or not the improvement is in areas involving bringing his or her faith across the secular–sacred divide; professional development such as is common in career development; or in personal areas such as raising children, managing finances, or strengthening marriages. The disciple, not the coach, knows best what he or she is facing. The coach's primary task is to enter into those situations to help the coachee as he or she moves forward to greater success and health. How is this shifted mindset practically accomplished?

The first step in achieving this mindset is for discipling coaches to come to the realization and firm belief that coaching, even DSC, is primarily about helping others in the process of making sense of past and current realities. The discipling coach comes to the relationship to help the coachee make sense of his or her own story.[5] This is largely due to the fact that peoples' actions are greatly influenced by how they perceive their own situation.[6] The coach's storytelling can be a huge part of this, as I have evidenced by sharing my own stories within this work, but it must also involve a great deal of storytelling and exploration by the coachee. Stories are objects of a sort. When properly explored, they can help coachees understand their internal motivations for the particular courses of action they took.[7] However, one of the dangers associated with storytelling is when the coach delves too deeply into *storyselling*.

Adrian Carr and Cheryl Ann argued storytelling and storyselling are both part of effective coaching dynamics; however, storyselling can become a problem when the coach relies too heavily on his or her own stories to unduly influence coachees toward a particular course of action the coach determines is best.[8] One of the best ways for discipling coaches to overcome the abuses associated with storyselling is to explore their own motivations for sharing—or not sharing—a particular story with a coachee. Before sharing a story, ask yourself: Is the story designed to help the other person understand his or her own actions, motivations, or feelings? Or is it designed to unduly influence the other person to take the steps you think are best in the particular situation? This is something I have to personally wrestle with on a regular basis in my paid coaching activities.

For instance, I was once told by a paid coaching client how he was not entirely satisfied with the coaching process thus far. My immediate reaction was to share a story with him about how another paid coaching client had felt the same way at a certain point but then later reversed his position as he came to understand how coaching had helped him move forward in his professional life. Before I shared this story, I asked myself what my internal motivation was for wanting to share this story. Was I trying to help this man get real value out of our coaching relationship? Or was I attempting to protect my income and reputation? I concluded self-preservation was my main motivator, which meant I should not share the story (even though I had permission from the other client). Instead of selling the other man's story, I needed to engage in active listening, prayer, and discernment as the coachee shared his story. While it might be appropriate to share the other man's story at some point in the relationship, at that time I had to avoid it because it was about my agenda and not the coachee's agenda.

A second way of uncovering the coachee's agenda is through a variation of powerful questioning in the form of direct questions. Before exploring the use of direct questioning, it is important to note that if questions are too abrupt, they can come across as uncaring, thus setting the relationship back.[9] However, with careful practice and discernment, direct questions can be a powerful force in uncovering the agenda a coachee needs to explore.

Christian coaching expert Gary Collins provided examples of direct questions:

- What brought you to coaching?

- What would you like to accomplish in coaching?

- What major things are happening in your life right now?

- How would you like your life to be different one year from now?

- As we work together, what are some ways in which I could be most beneficial to you?

- What should I avoid because it would not be beneficial?[10]

While these questions may seem too short and direct to be of much value, I have discovered their use has often had a profound impact. This has been especially true in my paid coaching when it focuses on assisting people with career transitions. The unspoken assumption of coaching engagements is they will always focus on helping people to move from one position to another; however, this is not always what the coachee needs in the moment. One session I spent with Kenneth illustrates the point.

During a meeting with Kenneth, I was especially attentive in my listening. About 20 minutes into the session, Kenneth was agitated, but I did not know why and did not want to assume. I stopped and asked him, "What else can I help you process today?" He immediately responded with a tone of voice that changed from agitation to relief: "Jerry, I know you are a man of faith, and I am too. However, I am struggling deeply right now with the uncertainty associated with finding a new job. What I really need is to ask you if you will pray for me." I was delighted to respond affirmatively that I *had* been praying for him and would continue to pray for him. I even asked if he would allow me to pray *with* him right then and there. The prospect of praying with me slightly unnerved him, but he decided it would be beneficial to move past his discomfort and pray together. By the end of our session, Kenneth had renewed faith that God was in control of his career transition, and he was ready to go to work again in pursuit of his goal of gaining a new position with a new company. All of this came about because I was willing to stop and ask a direct question about what would help Kenneth the most during the remainder of our time together.

A third way to uncover the coachee's agenda is through establishing goals the coachee will pursue between sessions and a plan for accountability regarding those goals. Goal agreement with accountability catalyzes action and attention, especially if the goal is time bound.[11] When the coachee sets a goal and agrees to be accountable for the goal, it sets the agenda for future meetings. One of the best strategies for setting goals I have used is the GROW framework, which is explored in more detail in the next chapter. However, let's look at an example of how this might work.

Richelle was a member of a church I was pastoring. She had sought my help. For a few years, she had been involved with a parachurch organization that ministered to youth in the area where we lived. Her love for the organization and the young people it ministered to had served to spark her greater involvement. At the peak of her activity with the organization, Richelle had allowed herself to be nominated and elected as the board president. The pressure this brought in her life was causing her to struggle to meet all of her commitments at home, work, church, and the organization. Richelle questioned whether or not she had gone too far in accepting the position as president. As we processed this together, she became convinced it was in the best interest of everyone involved that she step down as the president, trusting God to provide an appropriate replacement in her absence. As we explored this option, we agreed on a timetable for her resignation as president, the steps needed to ensure a smooth transition, and a plan of accountability to make sure she followed through. The plan of accountability involved setting agendas for our subsequent times together to discuss her progress in executing the plan. Simply agreeing to include these items in our subsequent meetings kept Richelle on track and enabled her agenda to come to the forefront. Before long, Richelle had executed all of the steps she had designed, and both she and the parachurch organization are in much healthier places to continue moving forward.

A final area to be discussed here that greatly helps in the coachee setting the agenda is closely related to direct questioning but with a slight twist. It involves regularly asking coachees, "In what ways am I, as the coach, hindering you from pursuing your goals or otherwise derailing the process?" On the surface, this question seems dangerous because it has the potential to degrade the coachee's trust in the discipling coach. However, I have discovered that by putting my ego to the side, admitting I do not have all the answers, and asking the question, people find greater levels of empowerment in the DSC process.

In *Co-active Coaching*, the authors argued such times of vulnerability on the coach's part facilitate a more collaborative relationship between the parties involved. The intentional blurring of the lines of the leader–follower relationship into a more participative process builds trust rather than destroys it.[12] While it can be daunting for a discipling coach to be so vulnerable, it usually causes the coachee to respond with his or her own increased vulnerability and openness in future DSC sessions. Let's return to Larry's story to see how many of these techniques can be utilized to effectively engage disciples in setting the agenda for DSC relationships.

Larry's Story Revisited

At the conclusion of Chapter 5, Larry's story touched briefly on his views of money and biblical stewardship. During the early years of Larry's faith, he had been exposed to some false teaching about how tithes and offerings worked. Because of this teaching, he had believed the more money he gave to the church, the more money he would receive as a blessing from God. This brought Larry and his wife to the place where they had no choice but to file for bankruptcy. As I worked with Larry through this time, I constantly found myself wanting to give him advice on how to get out of his financial predicament. The truth was he did not want this advice. He wanted someone to pray with him, empathize with his situation, and help him not repeat the same mistakes. I largely failed in this because I was so certain I had the answers for him.

Eventually, Larry and his wife dug themselves out of the hole they had created, and things seemed to be going well for them. They bought a new house, Larry came on staff of the church, and the ministry moved forward. Then there came a day when we were doing a mini-audit of the church's books and discovered something was amiss. Larry's wife had been serving as the church treasurer for a short stint. I went to her to discuss the discrepancy in the books. She confessed that she had been mishandling some of the church's finances and covering it up. Specifically, their family tithes and offerings were not being deposited in the church's accounts as our records indicated. Instead, because they were beginning to get into financial trouble again, she had been taking back their tithe from the church without Larry's knowledge to cover their personal bills. Upon this revelation, Larry immediately made it right with the church, his wife was removed from anything to do with church finances, the whole thing was publicly confessed and repented of, and a plan of restoration was put in place. However, more needed to be done in our DSC conversations to help Larry grow.

As I used all of the skills outlined in the DSC model, it became apparent a particular agenda needed to dominate our coaching times together. I thought it should involve financial management classes. But this was not what was needed. As I prayed for Larry, directly questioned him, and actively listened, Larry deemed what was really needed for our coaching time was to focus on him being a better husband and partner to his wife. For their entire marriage, Larry had been the care-free guy who put all the pressures of running the household on his wife. Larry expected that when he wanted something, no matter what the cost, his wife needed to get creative to make sure they could support it. Even though I initially thought financial management was the problem that should define our coaching agenda, a biblical view of marriage is what Larry decided he actually needed help on.

Larry's agenda for our coaching was spot on. As I served in a discipling coach capacity for Larry, his marriage flourished in ways it never had before. Larry's wife was free from the crushing pressure of managing their house while Larry served at church. In our sessions together, we employed the GROW framework to set *goals*, take stock of current *reality*, look objectively at the *opportunities and obstacles* associated with those goals, and design a *way forward*. Part of this involved Larry wanting a plan of accountability designed to help him stay on course in his marriage. Again, what I believed to be a finance problem was really a marital problem, and this would have gone unaddressed had I not allowed Larry to set the agenda for our DSC relationship as I helped him grow and develop. This is why it is so important to trust the coachee. The coachee usually knows much better than the coach what he or she needs.

---

1 Bence, P. A. (1998). *Acts: A Bible commentary in the Wesleyan tradition.* Indianapolis, IN: Wesleyan Publishing House, p. 95.

2 Christian Coaches Network International has developed a white paper on the subject of the distinctions of Christian coaching as opposed to secular coaching (see https://christiancoaches.com/wp-content/uploads/2017/10/CCNI-Christian-Coaching-Distinctions.pdf). One of the primary distinctions is the reliance on the Holy Spirit as an active participant in the coaching process.

3 Talbert, C. H. (2005). *Reading Acts: A literary and theological commentary on the Acts of the Apostles* (Rev. ed.). Macon, GA: Smyth & Helwys, p. 77.

4 Fee, G. D., & Hubbard, R. L., Jr. (Eds.). (2011). *The Eerdmans companion to the Bible.* Grand Rapids, MI: Cambridge, UK: William B. Eerdmans Publishing Co.

5 Reissner, S. C., & Angélique, D. T. (2011). Power and the tale: Coaching as storyselling. *The Journal of Management Development, 30*(3), 247–259.

6 Carraway, J. H., & Young, T. (2015). Implementation of a districtwide policy to improve principals' instructional leadership: Principals' sensemaking of the skillful observation and coaching laboratory. *Educational Policy, 29*(1), 230–256.

7 Ann, C., & Carr, A. N. (2011). Inside outside leadership development: Coaching and storytelling potential. *The Journal of Management Development, 30*(3), 297–310.

8 Carr, A. N., & Ann, C. (2011). The use and abuse of storytelling in organizations. *The Journal of Management Development*, 30(3), 236–246.

9 Ulrich, D. (2008). Coaching for results. *Business Strategy Series*, 9(3), 104–114.

10 Collins, G. R. (2002). *Christian coaching: Helping others turn potential into reality* (2nd ed.). Colorado Springs, CO: Navpress, p. 105.

11 Disbennett-Lee, R. (2005). *A study of international life coaches on the skills and strategies used during the coaching process*, City, ST: Publisher, p. 75.

12 Kimsey-House, H., Kimsey-House, K., Sandahl, P., & Whitworth, L. (2011). *Co-active coaching: Changing business, transforming lives*. Boston, MA: Nicholas Brealey, p. 187.

CHAPTER 8

Utilizing the GROW Framework

On their return the apostles told him all that they had done.
And he took them and withdrew apart to a town called
Bethsaida. When the crowds learned it, they followed him, and
he welcomed them and spoke to them of the kingdom of God
and cured those who had need of healing. Now the day began
to wear away, and the twelve came and said to him, "Send
the crowd away to go into the surrounding villages and coun-
tryside to find lodging and get provisions, for we are here in a
desolate place." But he said to them, "You give them something
to eat." They said, "We have no more than five loaves and two
fish—unless we are to go and buy food for all these people."
For there were about five thousand men. And he said to his
disciples, "Have them sit down in groups of about fifty each."
And they did so, and had them all sit down. And taking the
five loaves and the two fish, he looked up to heaven and said a
blessing over them. Then he broke the loaves and gave them to
the disciples to set before the crowd. And they all ate and were
satisfied. And what was left over was picked up, twelve baskets
of broken pieces. (Luke 9:10–17)

While discipleship style coaching (DSC) largely relies on the disciple or coachee to set the agenda during encounters, it does not mean the discipling coach is inactive during the process. To the contrary, the discipling coach has a critical role to play with coachees: help them take stock of their current reality, set goals to help them move from where they are to where they want to be, design plans that make the best use of the opportunities available while overcoming obstacles, and provide encouragement and accountability. Discipling coaches use a myriad of frameworks in this process. I have found the acrostic GROW greatly helps me to remember what needs to be done as I work with individuals. This acrostic is powerful and effective for two reasons.

First, the letters stand for the main points people need to consider when planning. The G is for goal(s). It reminds both the coachee and coach that a goal must be set. The R stands for current reality. It encourages the discipling coach to help the coachee explore the reality of his or her current situation in light of where he or she wants to go. The O stands for obstacles and opportunities. I need to help a coachee consider what things stand in his or her way and how those obstacles can be turned into opportunities to achieve the goal in mind. Lastly, the W stands for way forward. It reminds both the coach and the coachee that goals will likely not be accomplished unless there is an action-oriented and time-sensitive plan established to achieve them.[1] While the framework this acrostic represents is simple, it is also powerful in helping people move forward. This becomes apparent when we consider how Jesus employed the principles it represents with his disciples as 5,000 people (not including women and children) were fed with five loaves of bread and two small fish.

THE PASSAGE EXPLORED

All four gospel writers retold the feeding of the 5,000 in their individual accounts of Jesus' life and ministry. While each retelling reveals different nuances of what happened that day, Luke's version of the events is most salient in demonstrating how Jesus employed the principles embodied in the GROW framework to help his disciples accomplish something spectacular. In most Bible translations, this passage is labeled to indicate Jesus did the feeding. However, Luke 9:16 indicates it was not Jesus who did it but the disciples who accomplished this great miracle as Jesus came alongside of them in an empowering way. One noted theologian and scholar, N. T. Wright, wrote, "Jesus *invites the disciples into partnership here by telling them* [emphasis added] to give the crowds something to eat."[2] Verse 16 indicates the miracle took place in the disciples' hands as *they* distributed the broken loaves and fish Jesus returned to them. Do not let this fact escape your notice. Jesus, by the power of the Spirit, provided the blessing and empowerment. But it was the disciples who actually enacted the plan by distributing the food.

The truth of this narrative was first revealed to me via a DVD teaching called *The Blessed Life* by Pastor Robert Morris.[3] Pastor Morris drew attention to the fact the miracle took place in the disciples' hands after Jesus had taken what they offered, blessed it, broke it, and gave them back less (i.e., the broken pieces). In other words, Jesus did not feed the 5,000 for them; he helped them to feed the massive crowd via his expert guidance and the power of the Spirit of God. How does this encounter fit the GROW framework?

In the beginning of Luke 9, we learn Jesus had recently sent his disciples on a missionary journey to preach the coming kingdom of God. Upon their return, they were weary and worn and needed time to rest. Jesus took them away to the region of Bethsaida for a retreat. However, the crowds of people—who could not get enough of this new teaching—would not let these leaders rest. They followed them in an effort to receive more. Jesus, full of compassion and a zeal for the kingdom, obliged the crowd by continuing to teach them. In the process, Jesus and the disciples spent another full day ministering to the crowd in word and deed.

As the day wore away, the disciples approached Jesus and tried to convince him to dismiss the crowd so that they could get much-needed food and rest. Jesus challenged the disciples' thinking by planting the idea in them that they still had more to give. As the disciples considered this thought or new goal, they took stock of their current reality. The truth was, they only had the borrowed lunch of a small boy—five loaves of bread and two small fish—with which to accomplish such a feat. The obstacle, as the disciples saw it, was insufficient food to feed the crowd and/or lack of funds to buy the provisions. Jesus did not see these obstacles. He encouraged the disciples to view their seeming lack of resources as an opportunity for God to show off.

Pastor Morris posited how he thought the disciples figured something out in this encounter. He believed the disciples assumed Jesus was going to perform a miracle involving multiplying the food akin to that recorded in 1 Kings 17 and 2 Kings 4. However, Jesus did not do this. Jesus was interested in helping the disciples accomplish the work of the kingdom. He helped the disciples develop a plan to organize the people in groups of about 50. He then prayed over what little they had, invoking the blessing of God on it and breaking the food into smaller pieces, and challenged the disciples to give it away. The disciples were probably not prepared for this, but Jesus believed in them (as discipling coaches should). Jesus urged them to trust they had access to the needed resources to achieve the unachievable.

The disciples began to distribute the food. As they did this, it multiplied in their very hands. It multiplied so much, eventually everyone ate their fill and 12 baskets of leftovers were collected. The miracle itself happened as the disciples embarked on the way forward they designed with Jesus' help. What if the disciples had not followed through with the action steps of distributing the food? But they did! This was possible because Jesus believed in them. They could help the crowd—as well as themselves—cross the secular–sacred divide and see the miracles of the kingdom come. Jesus helped them set a goal of caring for the people, take stock of the seemingly bleak reality they were facing, clearly see the obstacles that needed to be overcome (i.e., lack of food and lack of faith), turn those obstacles into opportunities, and then make a way forward by developing an action plan and subsequent timetable. My use of the GROW framework has not seen results this dramatic, but the results have been spectacular in their own right. The individuals I have worked with have overcome insurmountable odds and moved forward in their professional and personal lives. Often, this has involved an accompanying growth in their personal faith as they crossed the secular–sacred divide to bring kingdom principles and living into their everyday lives.

EXPLORING THE GROW FRAMEWORK IN DEPTH

While the feeding of the 5,000 as recounted by Luke illustrates how the GROW framework can be effective in helping people, discipling coaches must explore it in depth if they are to use it. One of the most important aspects of the effective use of

GROW is realizing this is not simply another step in the DSC process. It is part of a wholistic approach built on the foundational skills we have already discussed. Discipling coaches cannot substitute the GROW framework for viewing everyone as a potential disciple, making extensive use of prayer in DSC relationships, developing strong listening and questioning skills, and allowing the coachee to set the agenda. The GROW framework is to be employed *while* utilizing the other mindsets and skills of the DSC model. This becomes apparent as each aspect of GROW is unpacked and practical examples are given.

As mentioned, G stands for goal. One of the common characteristics of all solution-focused coaching models, including the DSC model, is the insistence of helping a coachee define the future desired state and to construct a pathway in both thinking and action designed to help him or her achieve it.[4] The GROW framework helps enable this by drawing immediate attention to the need for defining (and subsequently refining) the desired end state by highlighting the goal-focused nature of the DSC model. The adage "If you aim at nothing, you will hit it every time" is meant to describe what happens when individuals or groups fail to set tangible goals. GROW seeks to avoid this. However, simply setting a goal is not enough. This is made clear by the passage in Luke as the disciples set their initial goal.

In the moment, the disciples initially set a goal to care for people by sending them on their way to find food and shelter. However, this goal failed to account for the reality the people (and the disciples) faced, as well as the obstacles and opportunities present. Jesus stepped in to gently challenge the disciples' basic assumptions in order to help them refine their goals. This is important because initial goals are often refined (and even replaced entirely) as the GROW framework is utilized.

This helps us to realize, as discipling coaches, goal defining is first in the process, but it is also continuous throughout the process as the reality of the situation, obstacles, and opportunities are assessed. Discipling coaches and coachees should not assume the G of GROW is completed once an initial goal is set. The goal must initially remain flexible and only become solid as action steps are developed when utilizing W to design a way forward. "Bearing this process in mind the GROW [framework] . . . might be more accurately represented as GRGROGROOGROWOGORW!"[5] How are initial goals most effectively set and then further refined?

The first step is by powerful, yet simple, questioning to uncover what the coachee wants to accomplish in his or her time with the discipling coach.[6] Ask a coachee, "What would you like to accomplish as a result of our time together today?" Oftentimes, the coachee will vaguely define a goal or purpose for the DSC session, and this is acceptable. This type of ambiguous goal setting happened frequently in my sessions with Chrissy, who oversaw the adult discipleship ministries at the church. Chrissy came to our times together with only a gnawing apprehension that what she was trying to accomplish was not working and needed to change. One particular meeting illustrates this point.

Chrissy arrived a bit flustered because she could not get all of the video technology for the church's discipleship program working in all the rooms of the facility. When I asked her what she wanted to accomplish together in our session, she had no answer. She knew getting the technology working was crucial to implementing her plans, but she was at a complete loss as to how she could move forward because she lacked the necessary technical skills. As I actively listened to her with my eyes and ears, prayed and listened for the Holy Spirit to respond, and employed open-ended questions, she confessed her inadequacy to make things work. Part of what led her to this conclusion was that she took stock of her own *reality* in technical aptitudes needed to make the program succeed. She determined a major *obstacle* for success is one she could not overcome on her own. I asked her how she could turn this obstacle into an *opportunity* to involve others.

As we talked about this, Chrissy realized she would have to enlist other organizational members in the process, and she identified some potential candidates. As we discussed this over the course of an hour, Chrissy finally defined her *goal* specifically as enlisting the help of James to get the network stabilized for a full-scale deployment. She determined actionable steps and a timetable to make her *way* forward to accomplish her *goal*. She left the meeting feeling empowered because she had a sense of direction. While this process sounds linear, it is not. It more closely resembled GRGROGROOGROWOGORW than it did GROW. This story illustrates the initially flexible nature of goals and the need for a discipling coach to avoid rigidly adhering to a four-step process—moving back and forth along the GROW framework as needed.

This is important to note because of the increasing popularity of SMART goals. Although there are numerous interpretations for what the letters in SMART signify, I define them as specific, measurable, agreed-upon, realistic, and time-based.[7] This way of understanding goals can be extremely helpful in the goal-setting process, but this must occur at the end of a DSC session and not in the beginning. It is also important to mention goals are often further refined as the GROW process is repeated in subsequent sessions because implementing the way forward may reveal other opportunities and obstacles that must be taken advantage of or overcome. For instance, Chrissy found after her initial meeting with James that the timetable needed to be changed as James assessed the network, researched other equipment needed to stabilize the network, and secured money from the budget to procure the equipment before it could be installed. This naturally leads us to the R of the GROW framework.

As previously noted, R stands for the need to take stock of the reality of the situation a coachee is facing. In my experience as a professional coach, business leader, and pastor, groups and individuals often fail to take adequate stock of their current situations as they make plans to address the issues they are facing. Discipling coaches can be of great assistance as they keep coachees grounded in reality. This occurs as discipling coaches use the skills of active listening, powerful questioning, and the discipline of prayer to help the coachee consider all factors affecting his or her current situation as well as consider alternative viewpoints. One area in which this has been especially helpful is when coachees are dealing with interpersonal relationships with their coach.

In the book *Crucial Conversations: Tools for Talking When Stakes are High*,[8] the authors highlighted the need to consider alternative views to a situation in the process of making sense. This is because of the human propensity to attribute incorrect motives to others for their behaviors and then act upon the situation based on the faulty assumption. However, reality checking and sense making do not start and stop with others. This is only one step in the process.

Effective discipling coaches are also able to assist others via the skills outlined in DSC by helping coachees to question their taken-for-granted, basic assumptions; explore how fear and insecurity might be affecting a given situation; and even question whether time-tested paradigms are still relevant in the current environment.[9] Taking stock of the current reality is not just about questioning negative beliefs or self-talk. It is also about helping those who are overly optimistic gain a better understanding on their current reality as well. To illustrate this, let's consider Reginald's story.

Reginald contracted with me for paid coaching services as he looked to transition in his career. At our first session, something he said set off alarm bells within me. Reginald had shared his expectation that with my help he could find a new role in a new company as a vice president in under 30 days. While his confidence in my abilities as a coach was flattering, I knew this was not a realistic goal. While I had, in the past, helped people transition this quickly, much of that had to do with them simply being in the right place at the right time. I shared widely published career transition statistics for executives with Reginald to give him a more realistic viewpoint. Reginald was unwilling or unable to change his expectations. The unrealistic assumptions he deeply held left me with no choice but to refund his money and terminate the contract. However, all was not lost in this encounter. I was able to share with him my faith, commit to pray for him, and even meet with him outside of a formal coaching engagement as he went through his transition. Reginald came face to face with the reality of his situation and accurately assessed the obstacles and opportunities it presented. He is now happily working in a new career.

Reality checking is so important in the DSC process because it naturally leads individuals to consider both the obstacles and opportunities of a given situation—O of the GROW framework. Identifying obstacles can start as simple as asking the question, "What do you see as obstacles that are blocking your from achieving your goal?"[10] While this may seem overly simplistic, it is a good approach in helping a person consider what challenges he or she might face as he or she pursues a goal. Furthermore, it can be used to refine goals when obstacles are identified that are insurmountable at the current time.

I used this technique with Stephanie, a paid coaching client, who was looking to transition into the cruise industry as a cruise director. As we talked about the goal, Stephanie conducted some research on cruise director salaries and discovered they averaged far below what she needed to have to pay her bills. She realized the goal was not a good one and pursued other avenues. I asked what obstacles there were. She confessed she did not know the salary range and was concerned it might not be enough.

Identifying opportunities is also part of the GROW framework. Assessing opportunities should not be restricted to only identifying unseen boons. While discovering these things can be encouraging, opportunities also present themselves in the form of areas where the discipling coach can assist the coachee in his or her personal development.[11] For instance, Bryan was looking for a chance to move forward in his current company. As he considered his current reality, he identified a major obstacle for moving forward—he had not finished his undergraduate degree. While this obstacle threatened to overwhelm him and derail the coaching process, he decided to explore the opportunity of returning to school and finishing. As of this writing, he is about to graduate with his degree, and his professional life is looking up as a result. This was only because he assessed reality, identified obstacles and opportunities, refined his goal, and developed a plan to move forward. In Bryan's story, the *way* forward started with exploring returning to school to finish his degree. This is the W of the GROW framework—the final piece discipling coaches must help coachees to consider.

Goal attainment is a critical outcome that must be accomplished if coaching, even the DSC model, is going to gain popularity as a method of helping others in their developmental process. The good news is coaching methodologies have been shown to have significant impact as coaches assist others in this area.[12] This is why W is an important part of the GROW framework that must be effectively employed. Without specific, measurable, agreed-upon, realistic, and time-based goals that are action-oriented, goal attainment is unlikely. It is important for coaches to remember planning a way forward must maintain a careful balance between how the coachee desires to move forward and the accountability and the encouragement a discipling coach provides. If this balance is not maintained, one of two possible negative outcomes can happen.

The first negative outcome is the coachee does not make any noticeable progress on his or her goal. This can happen if the discipling coach is lax for one reason or another on providing encouragement and accountability. These two items are different but closely related. Encouragement can come in the form of offering congratulations and cheering a coachee along. Accountability is primarily accomplished by the discipling coach pointing out steps the coachee agreed to take when developing the way forward that have not yet been completed.[13] One of the main techniques I use to ensure I am not lax in this area is coming to clear agreement on the goal, including what steps need to be completed before the next meeting together, writing out the goal and steps, and providing a copy to both parties. In the next meeting, I go over the progress with a coachee as the first order of business.

A second negative outcome is the coach driving the process by taking accountability too far. This can happen if the discipling coach begins to either take responsibility for the coachee's action steps or allows the coachee to transfer that responsibility to the coach. In my experience, the second negative outcome of driving accountability too far is the more prevalent of the two. While something about my particular personality most likely causes this to some degree, there are other reasons this can happen.

This happened more frequently for me in the more formal coaching arrangements I have been involved in, especially those in which I am paid. Early on, I found one of the main reasons this was happening was because the formal coaching agreement I used was not clear enough in spelling out what each party would bring to the relationship. To overcome this, I began using more clearly worded written agreements that require coachees to both sign it at the end and to place their initials next to key points indicating that the results of coaching, especially goal attainment, are in the hands of the coachee. This does not mean I am not responsible to assist them. However, it does mean the coachee, not the coach, is ultimately the one responsible for the outcomes of the DSC engagement.

A second tool I have found helpful in avoiding transference of responsibility is the use of written quality assurance checks to be used periodically throughout the engagement lifecycle. The quality assurance forms have been instrumental in helping me to detect transference, whether on my part or the coachee's part, and stop it from happening much earlier. Written forms such as I describe do not work in informal DSC engagements because, by their very nature, informal engagements do not use forms. This causes me to be much more attentive to transference of responsibility in those situations. This is important to address because my heart is to see DSC used by both professional discipling coaches (with formal agreements in place) and nonprofessional discipling coaches (with no formal agreements).

How can discipling coaches who engage in the DSC process on an informal basis best avoid transference of responsibility? The first step is for the discipling coach to understand the real nature of accountability. Jerry Bridges, author of *The Pursuit of Holiness,* argued genuine accountability is not about forcing another to follow through, it is about asking the appropriate questions to cause him or her to think about what steps have or have not been taken and give an accounting of why.[14] Understanding accountability in this way helps release the discipling coach from feeling responsible for making a coachee progress toward the goal.

The apostle Paul succinctly expressed this principle in Galatians 6:5: "For each will have to bear his own load." This truth sets the discipling coach free as he or she rests in the idea that the coachee is responsible for his or her own progress according to the word of God. Once the coach has embraced this, he or she is able to help the coachee come to the same realization. How does this happen without formal, written agreements?

The best way I have found for this to occur is by ensuring I have regular and candid conversations with those I am coaching, pointing out how they are responsible for their own progress. In these conversations, I assure coachees I am in this with them, I will continue to provide the resources at my disposal, I will pray for them, and I will cheer them on. I also ask them to tell me in their own words who is responsible for what in the relationship, making sure to actively listen for clues that indicate they believe I am responsible for their progress. Sometimes the clues are direct, such as when a coachee asked me to approach someone for them to smooth over an argument. At other times, they are subtler, like when coachees have complained how my help has not been able to get them moving in the right direction. In all such instances, I stop coachees and directly address who is responsible for progress—them.

Unfortunately, the above tactics do not always work. In these instances, I have had to back out of the DSC relationship with coachees based on their then-current inability to accept responsibility for their own progress. When I do this, I let the individuals know I am willing to begin again should they become willing to accept responsibility. In most instances, they eventually return to the DSC relationship with a renewed commitment to personal accountability. Backing out of the relationship is a form of accountability that is highly effective in helping coachees see they are responsible for their own progress.

On a final note about accountability in the informal DSC relationships, the longest running coaching relationship I have is with Larry. No formal coaching agreement has been put in place between Larry and me, yet we have been engaged in the DSC process for years. Throughout this time, I have seen Larry grow by leaps and bounds. These growth spurts have been in his personal life as he crosses the secular–sacred divide, his professional life, and his own times coaching others using the DSC model. We return to his story again to see how the GROW framework has been used in our relationship.

Larry's Story Revisited

I now share the part of Larry's and my DSC story that highlights how the GROW framework is much more akin to GRGROGROOGROWOGORW than a linear process. The issue at hand was the impending loss of a worship leader, which spanned a two-year period of Larry's life and ministry. It all began when Larry became aware of some issues in this staff member's life that potentially disqualified her from continuing in her role. As Larry and I engaged in the DSC process over the two years, the goal changed multiple times, as did the way forward. I believe this will help you understand how messy (yet beautiful) the coaching process can be.

When the issue with the worship leader first came to light, Larry had to deal with some critical issues required by his denomination because of their official position on church discipline and restoration. Larry's initial goal was to ensure he protected the church from any backlash that might arise as a result of his worship leader's problems being revealed. Through active listening, powerful questioning, and prayer, I helped Larry see there was more than one goal he needed to reach for. Protecting the church was important, but protecting his worship leader was also important. This included seeing her restored in the ministry.

As Larry wrestled through how this might happen, he took stock of his current reality. One obstacle was apparent—he did not have a ready replacement within the congregation to assume the role of worship leader. A second obstacle was how well loved the worship leader was; the possibility that removing her might cause people to leave the church. As Larry and I talked and prayed together, I felt the Lord nudging me to ask him, "Is there anyone in the congregation who has shown the potential to lead worship?" As Larry contemplated this question, he came up with a candidate. Getting this candidate ready was both an obstacle and an opportunity—it would take time to properly train and prepare the replacement (the obstacle), but it also allowed the current leader a way to continue ministering in a diminished capacity instead of being taken out completely (the opportunity).

As Larry worked through this with both parties, he designed a way forward that transitioned leadership to the potential next worship leader while providing a path of restoration for the former one. Larry and I continued to meet throughout this time and refined the goal several times, adjusting the way forward as new obstacles and opportunities presented themselves during the intentional reality checks. Coupled with the goal of providing a worship leader for the church was the goal of getting the outgoing worship leader the professional help she needed through a counselor. This two-pronged approach saw the requirements of the discipline and restoration policy met and, more importantly, saw the outgoing worship leader's soul cared for in a Christ-honoring way.

As the steps for discipline and restoration concluded, the worship leader was restored to ministry within the church, though she never again assumed full control of the worship ministries. Instead, she served on the worship team (leading at times) and found joy and fulfillment as she actively used her gifts in the body of Christ. However, things became convoluted as new obstacles presented themselves.

One major obstacle was the original worship leader's husband was upset because he felt like his needs were ignored in the process. As this became known, Larry intentionally engaged in the DSC process with this man. As they met together, the man shared his hurts and issues with Larry. Larry tried to get the man to define some type of end goal for their times spent together, but he never would. Larry and I spoke about this issue on several occasions, and we concluded the major obstacle stopping Larry from moving forward with the man was the man's unwillingness to accept any responsibility in the situation. Instead of being accountable for his own life, this gentleman wanted others to bear all the responsibility for him. In other words, his goal was to get others to see how they were to blame for his situation.

Rather than cutting off the DSC process with the other man, Larry renewed his efforts to help this man discover his own part in the issues, see the obstacles and opportunities before him, set a healthy goal, and then design a way forward. As they did this, the man's goals changed almost weekly. This flip-flopping of goals reignited turmoil in the original worship leader, and it started them down a process of her resigning all of her positions at the church and moving to another church within the community. Larry and I revisited his goal of protecting the church. Specifically, he was concerned with losing other congregation members upon her departure. As we talked together, Larry gave me permission to make several suggestions about how he might handle things; however, he never implemented any of those suggestions. Instead, they served as an impetus for him to develop his own SMART goal for seeing the couple transition out of the church.

In the end, the couple moved away from the church with minimal impact. However, the story does not end here. Restoration of both individuals was still on Larry's heart and mind, and as of this writing, he is currently working on a way forward that will make this happen. While it is unlikely they will ever return to the church full time, it is possible the relationships can be restored. Larry is focusing on that as he refines his goal and plan of action to see this happen. Throughout the process, Larry has been accountable every step of the way, and he has taken a healthy view of his personal responsibility. All of this was accomplished without a formal coaching agreement. It demonstrates how the DSC model can successfully be used informally. More than this, Larry's current elder board at the church acknowledged the growth they have seen in Larry over the two-year period. They continue to encourage him to press on as he engages in the DSC process both as a coachee and a discipling coach.

1 This acrostic is a modified version of the one presented by Collins, G. R. (2002). *Christian coaching: Helping others turn potential into reality* (2nd ed.). Colorado Springs, CO: Navpress, p. 198.

2 Wright, N. T. (2004). *Luke for everyone.* London, England: Society for Promoting Christian Knowledge, pp. 107–108.

3 Morris, R. (n.d.). *The blessed life: Simple secrets for achieving guaranteed financial results.* Life Outreach International.

4 Adams, M. (2016). ENABLE: A solution-focused coaching model for individual and team coaching. *Coaching Psychologist,* 12(1), 17–23.

5 Grant, A. M. (2011). Is it time to REGROW the GROW model? Issues related to teaching coaching session structures. *Coaching Psychologist,* 7(2), 122.

6 Paralikar, S. (2018). A 'SIMPLE' and 'NICE' mentor who enables his mentee to 'GROW.' *National Journal of Integrated Research In Medicine,* 9(2), 94–96.

7 Day, T., & Tosey, P. (2011). Beyond SMART? A new framework for goal setting. *Curriculum Journal,* 22(4), 515–534.

8 Patterson, K., Grenny, J., McMillan, R., & Switzler, A. (2012). *Crucial conversations: Tools for talking when stakes are high.* New York, NY: McGraw-Hill.

9 Angélique, D. T. (2007). Making sense through coaching. *The Journal of Management Development,* 26(3), 282–291.

10 Richardson, L. (1998). Five-minute sales coaching. *Training & Development,* 52(9), 53–57.

11 Janes, J. L. (2016). *The sensemaking experience of newly appointed district teacher leader coordinators: A case study.*

12 Grant, A. M. (2002). *Towards a psychology of coaching: The impact of coaching on metacognition, mental health and goal attainment.*

13 Norz, B. (2011). Coaching helps build great teams. *MLO: Medical Laboratory Observer,* 43(9), 28–29.

14 Bridges, J. (2006). *The pursuit of holiness.* Colorado Springs, CO: NavPress.

CHAPTER 9

The DSC Model Requires Intentionality

Now as they went on their way, Jesus entered a village. And a woman named Martha welcomed him into her house. And she had a sister called Mary, who sat at the Lord's feet and listened to his teaching. But Martha was distracted with much serving. And she went up to him and said, "Lord, do you not care that my sister has left me to serve alone? Tell her then to help me." But the Lord answered her, "Martha, Martha, you are anxious and troubled about many things, but one thing is necessary. Mary has chosen the good portion, which will not be taken away from her." (Luke 10:38–42)

Coaching of any type requires a great deal of intentionality for all parties involved. The International Coach Federation addresses this in Section A(2) of their core competencies for coaching.[1] Christian Coaches Network International also affirms this as they have adopted the International Coach Federation competencies and then added to them a set of Christian values meant to help guide Christian coaches as they apply coaching methodologies in a faith-based context.[2]

The issue, however, with both of these organizations is their assumption that coaching only takes place in a formal setting with a written coaching agreement and that coaching is a professional and often paid-for activity where people actively seek the help of a coach. Thus, a formal coaching agreement that includes setting a schedule for coaching sessions is needed. This assumption is further reinforced because both organizations offer credentialing programs for professional coaches. While having a formal agreement is not bad, it overlooks the possibility of using coaching methodologies in our everyday relationships as coaches seize coaching moments that present themselves. This is where the discipleship style counseling (DSC) model makes its biggest departure from coaching industry norms.

While intentionally scheduling coaching sessions, agreeing upon *homework* assignments, and following the formal coaching agreement do apply to the DSC model in formal engagements, DSC also supports seizing coaching moments in our everyday interactions with people we encounter. These moments are primarily facilitated by the discipline of prayer, especially listening prayer, as we hear the still, small voice of the Holy Spirit prompting us to engage in coaching behaviors with people we come in contact with. Jesus' interaction with two sisters, Mary and Martha, illustrates how this happens.

Before we explore the passage, let me make it clear that I am not against the core competencies presented by either the Christian Coaches Network International or the International Coach Federation. I adhere to their ethical guidelines in my formal DSC coaching engagements—both paid and unpaid. However, I believe coaching is such a powerful tool to transform people. We should not limit its use to formal settings.

Instead, we should embrace coaching moments in every area of life as the Holy Spirit presents us with opportunities to utilize the skills we have developed as discipling coaches.

THE PASSAGE EXPLORED

While Luke 10:38–42 does not include every aspect of the DSC model, it does include enough of the principles to be relevant. A particular area of interest, one many Western readers may overlook, is Mary sitting at the feet of Jesus. In Jewish culture, sitting at the feet of a rabbi like Jesus was a male role. It would have caused Martha to feel uncomfortable. This crossing of gender roles challenged Martha to the core because Mary should have—as a woman—been in the kitchen with her sister preparing the meal. This discomfort and interpersonal turmoil with her sister caused Martha to approach Jesus for help with her problem.[3] Jesus, however, did not take responsibility for solving Martha's problem. He challenged her to reconsider her goals, the social and personal obstacles she needed to overcome, the opportunity sitting at a teacher's feet would present, and *then* consider how she might make a way forward in light of all of this.

A second thing Jesus did not do was be offended by Martha's direct challenge of him. He reacted to her aggressive approach with grace, compassion, and mercy in a way that was meant to challenge her basic assumptions about what was going on.[4] He asked her to genuinely take stock of her current reality to open her to alternative viewpoints. In the process, he refused to allow her to transfer responsibility for solving her problem to him.

What is truly interesting is we do not know what Martha's ultimate reaction to Jesus' help was. Did she storm back to the kitchen to continue prepping the meal, did she sit down with her sister and engage with Jesus, or did she slink off in shame? We are not told. This is important for discipling coaches because the DSC process is solution-focused. As such, coaches tend to encourage—and even sometimes pressure—coachees to decide and plan a course of action. However, there are times when the best course of action is to allow coachees to contemplate the different perspectives we have helped them to see.

It has hopefully become apparent where Jesus utilized the principles embodied by the GROW framework in his encounter with Mary and Martha. We also know from studying the rest of Jesus' life and ministry how he was a disciplined man of prayer and was an active listener who used powerful questioning. It is also clear that Martha set the agenda for this encounter, which comports with the DSC model well. However, we are left with a question. Was this a coaching encounter that Jesus seized, or was it something else?

The easiest answer is to say it was not coaching, even DSC, for several reasons. First, coaching, even DSC coaching, was not a way Jewish people of this time period would have framed their interactions. Second, there was obviously no formal agreement between Martha and Jesus for coaching or any other type of service. Finally, if coaching had been a part of the Jewish context of this period, it would not have involved opposite-gender coaching relationships because of the strict gender roles in Israel at the time.[5] However, as our exploration of the passage has indicated, the encounter involved many of the DSC model principles discussed in previous chapters. As such, I assert this was a coaching moment Jesus seized upon as it presented itself, even though it was unscheduled and unplanned.

I realize this may be the most difficult shift in paradigms experienced coaches have to make to fully embrace the DSC model. It may even go too far for some coaching practitioners to ever accept, but it does not make it any less relevant because of that. My position throughout this work has been that DSC is less about becoming a professional coach and more about adopting a coaching lens through which discipling coaches can view all of their relationships. For those who adopt this new view, coaching opportunities (where discipling coaches can perfect their craft and help others along the way) are abundant. The numerous works that have been written on developing a culture of coaching inside organizations as small as family units[6] to multibillion-dollar corporations[7] support this assertion.

SEIZING THE COACHABLE MOMENTS

It is one thing to talk about setting regular schedules for coaching conversations, drawing up formal agreements for coaching engagements, and ensuring intentionality in every aspect of the relationship. It is another thing for discipling coaches to develop the requisite skills to seize coaching moments as they happen in their everyday interactions. If, however, coaching is to become a part of the culture of every organization a discipling coach is a part of, then coaches must learn how to identify and seize coaching moments, while modeling coaching behaviors for others. Strong DSC is not about titles, official roles, or formal recognition. It is about recognizing that as a discipling coach you can make a difference in others' lives by embracing opportunities as they are presented in the moment. This can happen whether you are a leader or follower. Coaching can be done from any chair at any time.[8]

The need to recognize coachable moments and seize them has been increasingly discussed. Companies like ExecVision are developing software and other tools designed to help people recognize coachable moments and act upon them before they slip away.[9] However, not every coachable moment can be identified by an automated computer program. At its core, coaching is a soft skill people must work hard to develop. Tom Daniels suggested all leaders, regardless of their level, must learn to coach; one of the most important aspects of this is learning to identify those coachable moments in others by active listening and discernment.[10] This is where the DSC model of coaching excels.

The reason for arguing the DSC model excels in identifying coachable moments by active listening and discernment is because the Christians utilizing this model have access to at least one resource non-Christian coaches do not—the third person of the trinity, the Holy Spirit.[11] Coaches who have trained their powers of discernment, as well as the skills of active listening and powerful questioning, through disciplined prayer are more in tune with the Spirit's nudging.[12] This attunement to the still, small voice of God helps discipling coaches more readily identify and act on coaching moments that were unscheduled. Jesus affirmed the reality of hearing God speak to us individually:

> *When the Spirit of truth comes, he will guide you into all the truth, for he will not speak on his own authority, but whatever he hears he will speak, and he will declare to you the things that are to come.* (John 16:13)

The reality of this is not some fanciful tale or wishful thinking; it is a promise from God to guide us in all of our interactions, including DSC.[13]

Beyond promising the Spirit would actively give us the words to say, along with the promptings to say them, Jesus modeled seizing coaching moments as well. One instance has been explored in Luke 10:38–42 with the recounting of Jesus while he was with Mary and Martha. This was also modeled in Luke 9:18–22 when Jesus questioned his disciples about who they thought he was, when he asked a group in Matthew 7:2 why they sought to remove the speck from a brother's eye when they had a log in their own eye, and when he asked in Mark 12:8 why the current generation was always seeking a sign. These were coachable and teachable moments where Jesus, led by the Spirit because of disciplined prayer and active listening, seized the moment and made an impact in those he was helping to grow. Can this type of in-the-moment coaching be powerful and transformative?

My personal experience has led me to conclude it can be, sometimes being more powerful than scheduled DSC sessions. Larry, who has been discussed at great length in previous chapters, recently confided in me that the most powerful coaching moments we have shared have come in unplanned, natural coaching moments occurring in the regular course of our conversations. Larry's testimony, however, could be dismissed as anecdotal. Is there any proof beyond such testimonies? According to research conducted by Carol Wilson,

> *Some of the most useful coaching in the workplace often happens in unscripted moments, such as a brief conversation at the coffee machine, or during a rushed phone call. Asking a useful question like "what would your ideal outcome be?" sometimes provides an avalanche of insight to someone who is stuck with an issue.*[14]

One reason informal and unplanned coaching is so effective is it is a form of informal learning focusing on the experiential and on development. This informal process helps individuals contextualize formal learning in a way that makes it stick with them.[15] It has even been documented that large majorities of people gain knowledge and skills better through informal means as opposed to formal ones,[16] which builds a strong case for implementing a practice of intentionally seizing coaching moments as they present themselves. How would this look in practice? To understand this, we return to various DSC coaching interactions.

Hank and Beth's Story

Serving as a pastor over the last 15 years has provided ample opportunities for both formal and informal DSC engagements. Some of the most rewarding moments came as I was able to intentionally seize coaching moments as they presented themselves. One example of this is the story of Hank and Beth.

Hank and Beth were members of a church I was serving in, and they were truly wonderful people. Both of them were—and still are—dedicated servants of God with a passion to reach the world with the gospel. In their zeal for the Lord, I was presented with many opportunities to engage in the DSC process as we talked over the challenges they were facing individually, as well as what we experienced together as a church.

One afternoon, Hank and Beth asked if we could meet and talk privately. The nudging of the Holy Spirit indicated to me there was a potential problem; I made scheduling this meeting a priority. When we met together, the couple shared with me the concerns they had with another member of the congregation and how he had been handling himself. As they opened up, they asked me for my assurance to keep the conversation just between us. As I paused to consider their request, the Holy Spirit prompted me to ask them, "Do you have an expectation that I will address the issue with the other party, or are you simply wanting to voice your concerns and get help moving forward?" They answered the latter was the case, and I agreed it would stay between us.

As they unpacked their grievance, I could understand their point of view; however, the conversation seemed to be more of a complaint session than something designed to help them move forward in a positive way. I asked them if they could define a goal—a desired outcome. As they wrestled with this question, they decided their goal was to help the other member change some destructive behavior if they could. As I listened with my eyes and ears to them (with one ear attuned to the Holy Spirit), I noticed they were increasingly uncomfortable with the idea of speaking to the other member on their own. As I internally prayed, the Spirit of God quickened in me the words of Matthew 18:15–20:

> *If your brother sins against you, go and tell him his fault, between you and him alone. If he listens to you, you have gained your brother. But if he does not listen, take one or two others along with you, that every charge may be established by the evidence of two or three witnesses. If he refuses to listen to them, tell it to the church. And if he refuses to listen even to the church, let him be to you as a Gentile and a tax collector. Truly, I say to you, whatever you bind on earth shall be bound in heaven, and whatever you loose on earth shall be loosed in heaven. Again I say to you, if two of you agree on earth about anything they ask, it will be done for them by my Father in heaven. For where two or three are gathered in my name, there am I among them.*

I asked them if they had considered this passage of scripture. They had not. We read the passage together. I asked them, "How does this passage apply to this situation?" Hank and Beth decided it applied because the other member had sinned against them and, as such, deserved to be confronted in order for forgiveness and reconciliation to happen. Over the next half hour, we talked about what this might look like.

With some careful questioning, intensive listening, and a lot of prayer, the couple concluded they should approach the other member in private first. We agreed if this proved fruitless, they would enlist one or two others who knew the situation firsthand. If taking along other witnesses did not work, they agreed it would be time to involve the church leadership.

I am unsure how their conversation with the other member went. They never brought it up again after that day. But I do think something positive happened, because they currently are speaking and fellowshipping with the other member again, and the relationship seems to be healed. The value of seizing this coachable moment with them is that I, as the pastor, was able to avoid Hank and Beth transferring responsibility for fixing the situation to me. Instead, they set their own goal, took a solid view of reality, processed the obstacles and opportunities, and designed actionable steps to make a way forward. This restored peace and harmony to the relationship with the other member, and everyone continued moving forward together as a unified church family.

Lucy's Story

Lucy was another person I was intentionally able to provide DSC. Lucy was an elderly widow in one of the churches I served in. As I got to know her, I found we both developed a great fondness and respect for one another. This relational tone set the stage for Lucy to share with me many of the personal struggles she had been facing since she moved to our area—one of which was in the area of her finances.

Upon moving to the area, Lucy quickly became financially overextended for a number of reasons. Chief among them was a medical issue that caused her to have to begin an expensive regimen of prescriptions to deal with her now chronic health issues. The prescription cost caused her not to be able to give to kingdom work the way she desired, and it eventually hampered her ability to pay her regular monthly expenses. The first time the issue came up, Lucy asked if the church could help her. The church policy was to help members like this one time with no questions asked; if subsequent help was needed, things would change.

In less than a month's time, Lucy returned to my office to request help a second time with her bills. As I prayerfully considered her request, the Holy Spirit brought to mind several times over the past month where Lucy had gone out to lunch with others. Interestingly enough, I was present at most of these meals. Each time I was there, someone had offered to pay for Lucy's meal because they knew the financial strain the prescription costs were putting on her. However, she refused to allow them to bless her in such a way. As this came to mind, I asked her if there were any areas in her life where she could cut expenses, to which she quickly replied there was not. To help her see some habits she had that contributed to her problems, I gently pointed out my observations over the past month. When I did this, Lucy became extremely agitated.

As we explored her agitation, she confessed to me how it made her feel like a beggar to have other people pay for her food. In short, her pride was getting in the way. At this point I asked her to consider if skipping these types of meals with people might be a viable alternative if she was not willing to let others buy her meal. She aggressively asserted it was not. I was surprised and almost pushed back on her. However, the Holy Spirit prompted me to overlook her insistence she must attend these types of functions, because the real issue had not yet been revealed. As I prayed in the moment, the Lord prompted me to ask her to write a list of all the medications she was taking. Lucy hastily jotted them down. I noticed something. She had written every prescription drug by its name brand.

This led to me asking Lucy why she had written down the name brands. She said she was taking the name brands instead of the generics because her doctor told her the generic versions would not work. Though I am not a student of medicine, I was surprised by this answer; however, my lack of medical knowledge was an obstacle to helping her. This is when it came to mind one of the church elders was a medical professional capable of reviewing her prescription list with her. Furthermore, Lucy and he were close friends. I asked her if she would be willing to meet with him and get his opinion. Lucy reluctantly agreed, and we set the meeting up.

During their meeting together, the church elder went over alternative choices for medicine with her. As they explored the many options, she agreed to change every prescription to a generic equivalent because of his assurances they would work just as well. In the end, Lucy's prescription costs were reduced from approximately $500 per month down to a mere $15. More importantly, she discovered the generics worked just as well as the name brands. All of this happened because I intentionally seized a set of coaching moments to help Lucy reach her goal of self-sustainment, overcome the obstacles and take advantages of the opportunities present in her reality, and make a way forward.

Jason's Story

Intentionally seizing coaching moments as they present themselves does not always have happy endings such as with Hank, Beth, and Lucy. Jason was an active and productive member of a church I was serving in. As I got to know Jason and his wife, I saw a great deal of potential in him as a future leader in the church. The Spirit prompted me to ask Jason if had ever considered becoming a church elder. Jason's face lit up when I asked this question because it was something the

Lord had laid upon his heart. As we talked about the goal, obstacles, and opportunities and designed a way forward, Jason and I came up with a plan of study and meeting together that would help him.

Over a period of several months, Jason completed every agreed-upon assignment ahead of schedule. Things seemed to be going well, and I seized several great coaching moments outside of our regularly scheduled meetings. One day, the Spirit prompted me to ask Jason: "Is there anything from your past that, if it came to light, would hinder your effectiveness as an elder?" I know the question landed because Jason's countenance immediately changed. Jason confessed to me there had been some infidelity several years back between his wife and another one of Jason's close family members. Though forgiveness and reconciliation had happened between Jason and his wife, there was still a lot of drama in the extended family surrounding the indiscretion.

The turmoil Jason was feeling about the situation prompted several meetings where we tried to work out a plan to bring final resolution to the issue. Although this was a major struggle for Jason, he was making good progress. His wife, however, did not. After a meeting Jason and I had, his wife showed up at church to give me a piece of her mind. She was certain the affair had no relevance on Jason serving as an elder, even though Jason thought it did. She demanded we let this drop and install Jason as an elder immediately. Jason did not agree. He believed the rawness of her emotions and the continued problems in the extended family were reasons to put becoming an elder on hold until the issue was resolved addressed adequately.

In response to Jason's and my decision, his wife went on a rampage. She contacted members of the church, began slinging mud, and caused the church to lose about 20% of its members before quitting the church herself. Even after Jason and his wife left the church, she continued her campaign of destruction until I was seized by a coaching moment with another of my elders. Bob confided in me that Jason and his wife had been meeting with their family privately to discuss their issues. As they did this, Bob and his wife were becoming increasingly upset. This is when the Holy Spirit prompted me to ask Bob why they were feeling this way. Bob concluded the reason for his consternation was due to the church he loved having the ranks of its membership decimated by controversy. This further prompted me to ask him how, if at all, he and his wife could stop it from happening again. In the end, Bob decided the Lord was leading him to confront Jason and his wife in a grace-filled manner in order to ask them to stop attacking the church. Amazingly enough, Jason's wife agreed, and the church eventually recovered.

While it may not seem prudent to share a story like Jason's, I believe it is important because discipling coaches need to know the DSC process will not always produce the results they desire. People are still people. They are unpredictable. However, amazing and transforming things often happen. Taking the chance to intentionally engage in the DSC process is well worth it—even when things go wrong. The rest of Larry's story and personal testimony in the next chapter serves as a final illustration to help you see how powerful and effective DSC is, as discipling coaches help others cross the secular–sacred divide and grow personally, professionally, emotionally, and spiritually.

1 See https://coachfederation.org/core-competencies for the core competencies set out by the International Coach Federation.

2 See https://christiancoaches.com/wp-content/uploads/2017/10/ Competencies-Edited-Final-2017.pdf for the modified Christian version of the ICF core competencies.

3 Wright, N. T. (2004). *Luke for everyone.* London, England: Society for Promoting Christian Knowledge, pp. 130–131.

4 Mills, M. S. (1999). *The life of Christ: A study guide to the gospel record.* Dallas, TX: 3E Ministries, Luke 10:38–42.

5 In his commentary on the passage, Wright (2004) pointed out how what Jesus and Mary were doing crossed those gender roles and blurred the lines so prevalent in Jewish culture by her sitting at a rabbi's feet learning.

6 Focus on the Family Canada (2013) published an article on parents adopting coaching behaviors with their children that serves as one example (see https://www.focusonthefamily.ca/content/ teaching-self-control-coaching-your-child-in-constructive-reactions).

7 Phillips, T. (2011). Creating a coaching culture across a global sales force. *Strategic HR Review,* 10(4), 5–10. This is a peer-reviewed article on how Microsoft strove to build a coaching culture across its global sales force.

8 Everyone's a coach. (2011). *Credit Union Management,* 34(1), 8.

9 ExecVision was awarded service provider of the year from the American Association of Inside Sales Professionals. (2018). *PR Newswire.*

10 Daniel, T. (2011). Leaders who coach. *Leadership Excellence,* 28(12), 12–13.

11 Christian Coaches Network International directly identifies the person and work of the Holy Spirit as one of the key distinctions for all forms of Christian coaching that gives Christian coaches an advantage over non-Christian interventions (see https://christiancoaches.com/wp-content/uploads/2017/10/ CCNI-Christian-Coaching-Distinctions.pdf).

12 Water, M. (1998). *Knowing god's will made easier.* Carlisle, UK: Hunt & Thorpe, p. 54.

13 While not specifically addressing coaching, Jesus further affirmed the truth of the active voice of the Spirit in Luke 12:11–12 when he said, "And when they bring you before the synagogues and the rulers and the authorities, do not be anxious about how you should defend yourself or what you should say, for the Holy Spirit will teach you in that very hour what you ought to say."

14 Wilson, C. (2011). Developing a coaching culture. *Industrial and Commercial Training,* 43(7), 413.

15 Becker, K., & Bish, A. (2017). Management development experiences and expectations: Informal vs formal learning. *Education & Training,* 59(6), 565–578.

16 Becker & Bish, 2017, 572.

CHAPTER 10

Larry's Testimony About the DSC Model

And they have conquered him by the blood of the Lamb and by the word of their testimony, for they loved not their lives even unto death. (Rev. 12:11)

Revelation 12:11 indicates the testimonies of those who have been touched by the power of the gospel are greatly effective in influencing others for the kingdom. This is true in all areas of life, and I believe it includes discipleship style coaching (DSC). That testimonies are powerful and effective is not some unfounded assertion. It has been proven in the Judeo–Christian scriptures and in the experience of untold millions of Christians worldwide.

Throughout this work, you have read the stories of many people and how they were positively impacted by use of the DSC model. I even presented the story of one man, Larry—from the time we started the DSC process together up until the present day. It was only yesterday when Larry and I had our latest DSC encounter with one another as we thought about what was most important to share in this book. The interesting issue with this is he was coaching me instead of me coaching him. That is the funny thing about a DSC relationship spanning 16 years—the lines sometimes get blurry on who is helping whom.

During our conversation, we were grappling with which of Larry's stories to share in Chapter 8. Larry profoundly said, "Jerry, you aren't going to like this, but the most powerful coaching times we have had together over the years are the times where we were just doing life together and you had a timely word of encouragement, an unexpected question to help me see things differently, or a direct challenge to my thinking." He did not know at the time how much I loved what he said because it affirmed the content of Chapter 9. Intentionally seizing coaching moments as they present themselves can literally change others and the world in which we live. So can sharing their testimonies.

I conclude this work with one of the most powerful testimonies of what DSC is capable of when it is done with regularity and intentionality. Much of what follows has been shared in bits and pieces throughout the preceding chapters. My goal is to help you see how all of those small stories—both victories and failures—came together to wreck Larry and me for Jesus and then empower us to go out and do it for others. Are you ready to see how Jesus makes beautiful things out of the messiness in our lives?

LARRY—A GUY WRECKED FOR JESUS . . . THEN SENT HOME

Before I bring Larry's story together for you in one coherent whole, I remind you of the goal I set at the conclusion of Chapter 1. My goal is *not* to help anyone become the best coach, discipler, or leader. Being a great helper to those you interact with will be a byproduct of my real goal. My true goal is to wreck your theology, your conceptions of God, even your methods of advancing the kingdom, and then send you home like the demoniac of Mark 5 to tell others all that the Lord has done for you. Then I want to help you explore ways you can disciple and coach others to do the same in order that the kingdom of heaven might fully come.

Being wrecked for Jesus, in a good way, and then empowered and released to see the same accomplished in the life of others is the goal of this book. For some of us, this means fully embracing the DSC model and implementing it in all of our coaching endeavors. For others, it means gleaning a few new principles of effective Christian coaching and adding it to our already substantial toolkit to help others grow and develop. Either way, the kingdom of heaven will be advanced as we help others who are attempting to cross the secular–sacred divide with kingdom principles and kingdom living. Larry is one such man. He does not do everything the way I would as a discipling coach. Instead, he applies the principles in the way that makes the most sense to him, and hundreds of people have been helped in the process.

The Beginning of Larry's Story

The real beginning of Larry's story happened before we ever met. In 1969, Larry was born to two loving parents, Richard and Lois Williams. Like most children of this era, Larry grew up in a home where Dad worked hard to provide for the family financially and Mom worked hard to take care of things at home. Also, like many of his generation, Larry's mother was a dedicated born-again Christian, while Dad was nominally in the faith. Larry grew up with one foot in the world and one foot in the church. The world's pull constantly threatened to crush the growing seed of the gospel his mother had so gently planted in his life. Like most of his friends, Larry grew up with all the things he needed and some of the things he wanted. Larry's life was comfortable, but it was not the way his mother wanted to see it.

To say Lois had a disciplined prayer life that included praying for Larry's salvation is an understatement. Like all believing mothers, she regularly sought the Lord through prayer and fasting, asking God to draw her son into the kingdom. After decades of prayer, Larry came to saving faith in 2001. This happened as Larry and his wife started attending Clarksville Alliance Church in a last-ditch effort to see their failing marriage saved. Reverend D. Wayne King visited the family in their home one evening to get to know them better. Larry's desire was to be nice—but not too nice. As a matter of fact, Larry offered his new pastor a beer to see if he could shock him. Because Wayne had a disciplined prayer life, he was not thrown off course.

Instead of letting Larry's offer of a beer stop the conversation, Wayne heard the Holy Spirit prompt him to pull out a little gospel tract called *Steps to Peace with God*. Larry was surprised by Wayne's use of this tool, as he thought such tactics were for little children. Besides, Larry thought he already knew Jesus. However, when they got to the scripture that talked about the wages of sin being death, Larry began to tear up and feel conviction like he had never felt any other time in his life. When Wayne showed an illustration in the book that showed a bridge between God and man that was made possible by Jesus' sacrifice on the cross, Larry knew he was still separated from God. For the first time ever, Larry realized he knew *about* Jesus, but he did not actually *know* him personally. That night, after a flood of silly questions, Larry gave his heart and life to Jesus for the first time, and Jesus began to make a beautiful wreck of Larry's life.

Larry was now saved by grace but still had a long way to go in his faith. His marriage was still a disaster, their finances were out of control, and life was dangling by a spider's thread. Multiple missional barriers, such as Larry being divorced and remarried, his socioeconomic status, his drug and alcohol use, and others, kept the church from effectively engaging in discipleship with Larry and his wife because they were expected to do all the work of crossing the missional barriers by becoming like everyone else in the church. This went on for several months before I met Larry when I started attending the church early in 2002.

In April 2002, I gave my life to Christ for the first time. Soon thereafter, I sensed the call of God on my life to enter into the ministry as a pastor. As I prepared for the ministry God had for me, Clarksville Alliance Church installed me as an associate pastor with the intention of using me to plant a daughter church. As the church members prayed about how they might best support this effort, Larry and his wife began to feel the Holy Spirit nudging them to join the church-planting team. This was in spite of the fact that neither family knew the first thing about planting a church.

By April 2003, we had launched Hopkinsville Bible Church in a neighboring community. Those days were full of excitement, anticipation, and a lot of hardship. God had given us a small team of nine people to plant a church, and every one of us was a babe in Christ. However, we made the best of what God was doing, and the church ultimately took off two years later when we moved back to Clarksville and changed our name to Crossroads Fellowship of the Christian and Missionary Alliance.

During those first two years, while we were still just a handful of people pursuing an impossible dream, God began to reveal to me the model I now call DSC. This first began when Larry crashed his company vehicle after he picked up his daughter from our house. This event was additionally traumatic because Larry's company required he submit to a drug screen immediately, and Larry had just smoked marijuana the day before. God used this event to show me how the church had been failing to cross the missional barriers to positively impact Larry and his family for the kingdom. Their lives were still highly compartmentalized, much of it being hidden from Christian friends. That was about to change.

As Larry helped me to write this final chapter, I asked him why he decided to start opening up to me at this point in time. While he did not have the capacity to realize it in the moment (or the language to explain it), Larry believes this was because I calibrated the invitation (the relationship) and the challenge (his personal responsibility) in a way no church person had ever done before. In other words, both of us were willing to trust that even though things were less than ideal, our relationship was strong enough to help us move forward as Larry committed to seek growth in the faith on a deeper and more profound level. However, things did not immediately become better. Some of them got worse.

Not long after, Larry stayed out all night with his boss on a booze bender. When Larry missed church the next day, his wife actually shared with my wife and me what truly happened. Larry, though, still tried to hide the fact by claiming he was sick. To his credit, it was not an outright lie. He had been up all night vomiting and suffered from a severe hangover the next day. Even though he tried to mislead me, I felt the Spirit nudging me to ask some pointed questions about his absence. Finally, Larry confessed his overindulgence in alcohol had gotten the better of him. He explained how he was lucky to be alive because he had driven home that night seeing triple images of everything.

As Larry recalls the story, it was the same time when he called me in fear and trembling because he believed he was going to go to prison for federal bank loan fraud. As we discussed what he was facing, I asked him, "Isn't it odd how something from years gone by can come back and haunt you?" Larry was not impressed with my question. In his mind, life was falling apart, and all I wanted to do was talk about how deception would eventually come back to bite you.

In a moment of frustration and desperation, my friend confessed his problem with alcohol, and we began the long process of setting a goal, checking reality, candidly looking at the obstacles and opportunities he was facing, and then designing a way forward for him to see his life turned around. While there is a part of me that would be proud to take the credit for what Larry accomplished as he worked past all of this, the credit does not go to me.

Larry was learning to take responsibility for his own life and actions, and I was learning to be a discipling coach who could rest in the truth that my coachee was the one who was best equipped to decide how to best move forward in his or her life. Those first two years of the church plant would see Larry face many more obstacles similar to this, but my love and respect grew for him as God revealed the kind of man Larry could become if I would simply commit to walking alongside of him in the DSC process.

Another item of interest is that during this two-year period of the church plant, I came to rely on Larry more and more as my right-hand man. Some people might find this shocking because of the issues Larry experienced, but I am certain God wanted me to continue loving him and allowing him to be used in the kingdom—even though it did not always make sense by human standards. The more Larry came to realize how much I valued him and believed in him, the more he opened up and made progress in every area of his life.

The Middle of Larry's Story

Once the church plant moved to Clarksville, Tennessee, we embarked on a journey of evangelism and outreach. Larry says this time in life is the one that had the most impact on him. We began to use the principles of evangelism taught by Ray Comfort and Kirk Cameron in *The Way of the Master*. These principles involved a lot of life on life as Larry and I hit the streets together to see the transforming power of Jesus take hold of people's lives. Over the years, Larry has consistently reminded me how powerful this time was because I trusted him enough to share life with him on the deepest levels. As a church planter who was now making my living as a full-time staff member, Larry could see how his part in our work together was having a significant impact on both the church and my family. For the first time in my life, I had a true brother whom I could trust to storm the gates of hell with me.

As Larry and I grew in our DSC relationship, I felt the Lord prompting me one day to ask Larry, "What would stop you from becoming a deacon in the church?" He was shocked by this question and quickly told me why it was a bad idea. I was not about to let his fear stop him from wrestling with the question. I asked him to commit to the discipline of prayer by taking this question to the Lord. God revealed to Larry all of the areas of his life where he had forbidden the Lord to come. In those moments, Larry could have chosen to turn back; instead, he yielded those areas one by one to Jesus. While I regularly coached Larry as he worked through these issues, I left the agenda of which ones to address (including the how and when) up to Larry because I believed in him. To say I would have chosen differently than he did would be an understatement, but being a discipling coach is not about getting people to do it my way. It is about trusting the Spirit of God in them to show the individual the best way to move forward.

Before long, Larry went beyond becoming a deacon by accepting an appointment as an elder in the church. From eldership, Larry became a youth pastor on staff. From there, Larry became the lead pastor of the church when I departed in 2010. Even though I left to replant another church, our DSC relationship did not stop. Larry and I continued to stay in contact, meeting regularly via telephone as I served as his discipling coach.

Turning the ministry of Crossroads Fellowship over to Larry was the key to seeing Larry develop his own set of skills as he employed the DSC model. The primary catalyst for this happening was when the Army transferred several of the elders at Crossroads at the same time. As Larry processed the loss of these godly men with me, he was tempted to take back all the leadership of the church. However, the Spirit of God prompted me to challenge his thinking. I remember asking him why his lack of preparation in training and growing new leaders was a valid excuse for taking full control of the church. The question cut to the heart of the matter with Larry, and it taught us both something powerful. The DSC process was not meant to work solely between two people. God intends to use this process to grow multiple generations of leaders who are equipped to cross the secular–sacred divide and bring king- dom principles to a lost and dying world.

Larry began adapting the principles he had learned as I coached him into a coherent model that would continue to reproduce healthy Christians. This happened as Larry invested his life in Christians and non-Christians alike. Along the way, Larry learned some painful lessons about becoming a discipling coach. Some of those lessons came in the form of failures. Some lessons came as he succeeded with people and then had to release them to serve in other cities around the country. Either way, God continued to get the glory as subsequent generations of discipling coaches were born.

Larry's Story Today

As you know from the many examples shared throughout this book, Larry does not always employ the DSC model in the way I would. However, he consistently engages as a discipling coach with friends, neighbors, family members, and coworkers. Some of these engagements are formal ones, those in which the person has consciously agreed to be coached. Some of them are informal, where Larry intentionally seizes the coaching moments God presents to him. The more disciplined Larry is in prayer, active listening, and asking powerful questions, the more effective he is as a discipling coach. But the road is not always easy, and sometimes he grows impatient with the process. One example is how he is employing the DSC model with his own son, Keith.

About four years ago, the relationship between Larry and Keith became strained to the point that Keith had to move out of his parents' home. During the first year or more, Larry and Keith rarely spoke, but this is not because Larry lacked a heart to see Keith grow in his faith and apply kingdom principles to life. It was because Larry and Keith had both fallen prey to the transference of responsibility that can sometimes happen as a coachee places the onus on the coach for achieving his or her goals. Keith blamed Larry for where he was in life, and Larry struggled with his own feelings of inadequacy to help his son become all God intended him to be. However, Larry committed to disciplined prayer for his son, and it was not long until God gave him a specific word for Keith.

While Larry was preaching through the beatitudes to the

congregation at Crossroads, God told Larry, "Love him!" Larry knew that he loved Keith, but God prompted Larry this was not enough. Keith did not need to be loved the way Larry wanted to love him; he needed to be loved the way he could personally receive it. Larry needed to believe in Keith and trust in the Spirit of God enough that he could reproduce the type of relationship Larry and I had stumbled onto as God revealed the DSC model to us.

We do not know how this story will end; however, the relationship between Larry and Keith has been restored, and they are back under one roof. While there is no formal coaching agreement, Larry is committed to praying for Keith, and he is longing for the day when he can pray with Keith again. The progress is slow with his son, but Larry believes that by using the principles outlined in the DSC model, his son will eventually cross the secular–sacred divide as Jesus wrecks him for the kingdom. Then Larry will be ready to teach Keith how to reproduce those results in the lives of others as God sends another son out to bring the transformative power of the kingdom into the lives of others.[1]

---

1 Chapter 10 was entirely written with Larry's involvement as we decided together the most salient points of the DSC model to share in his story.

REFERENCES

Adams, M. (2016). ENABLE: A solution-focused coaching model for individual and team coaching. *Coaching Psychologist, 12*(1), 17–23.

Anderson, D., & Anderson, M. (2011). *Coaching that counts: Harnessing the power of leadership coaching to deliver strategic value.* New York, NY: Routledge.

Angélique, D. T. (2007). Making sense through coaching. *The Journal of Management Development, 26*(3), 282–291.

Ann, C., & Carr, A. N. (2011). Inside outside leadership development: Coaching and storytelling potential. *The Journal of Management Development, 30*(3), 297–310.

Anonymous (2011). Everyone's a coach. *Credit Union Management, 34*(1), 8.

Anonymous. (2018). ExecVision awarded service provider of the year from the American association of inside sales professionals (AA-ISP). *PR Newswire.*

Becker, K., & Bish, A. (2017). Management development experiences and expectations: Informal vs formal learning. *Education & Training, 59*(6), 565–578.

Bence, P. A. (1998). *Acts: A bible commentary in the wesleyan tradition.* Indianapolis, IN: Wesleyan Publishing House.

Bounds, E. M. (1990). *The complete works of E. M. Bounds on prayer.* Grand Rapids, MI: Baker Books.

Brantley, M. E. (2007). *Executive coaching and deep learning* (Order No. 3255517). Available from ABI/INFORM Collection.

Brewer, W. F. (2001). Models in science and mental models in scientists and nonscientists. *Mind & Society, 2*(2), 33–48.

Bridges, J. (2006). *The pursuit of holiness.* Colorado Springs, CO: NavPress.

Bullock-Webster, G. R. (1912). Intercession. In G. Harford, M. Stevenson, & J. W. Tyrer (Eds.), *The Prayer Book Dictionary.* New York: Longman.

Cabal, T., Brand, C. O., Clendenen, E. R., Copan, P., Moreland, J. P., & Powell, D. (2007). *The apologetics study bible: Real questions, straight answers, stronger faith.* Nashville, TN: Holman Bible Publishers.

Calvin, J., & Owen, J. (2010). *Commentary on the epistle of Paul the apostle to the romans.* Bellingham, WA: Logos Bible Software.

Calvin, J., & Pringle, W. (2010). *Commentary on a harmony of the evangelists Matthew, Mark, and Luke.* Bellingham, WA: Logos Bible Software.

Carr, A. N., & Ann, C. (2011). The use and abuse of storytelling in organizations. *The Journal of Management Development, 30*(3), 236–246.

Carraway, J. H., & Young, T. (2015). Implementation of a districtwide policy to improve principals' instructional leadership: Principals' sensemaking of the skillful observation and coaching laboratory. *Educational Policy, 29*(1), 230–256.

Christian Coaches Network International. (2017). *Christian coaching competencies.* Retrieved from Christian Coaches Network International: https://christiancoaches.com/wpcontent/uploads/2017/10/Competencies-Edited-Final-2017.pdf

Christian Coaches Network International. (2017). *Definition of christian coaching.* Retrieved from Christian Coaches Network International: https://christiancoaches.com/wpcontent/uploads/2017/10/CCNI-Christian-Coaching-Distinctions.pdf

Collins, G. R. (2002). *Christian coaching: Helping others turn potential into reality* (2nd ed.). Colorado Springs, CO: Navpress.

Crane, T. G. (2017). *The heart of coaching: Using transformational coaching to create a high performance coaching culture* (4th ed.). San Diego, CA: FTA Press.

Daniel, T. (2011). Leaders who coach. *Leadership Excellence, 28*(12), 12–13.

Day, T., & Tosey, P. (2011). Beyond SMART? A new framework for goal setting. *Curriculum Journal, 22*(4), 515–534.

Disbennett-Lee, R. (2005). *A study of international life coaches on the skills and strategies used during the coaching process* (Order No. 3183531). Available from ABI/INFORM Collection. (305394901).

Fee, G. D., & Hubbard, R. L., Jr. (Eds.). (2011). *The eerdmans companion to the bible.* Grand Rapids, MI; Cambridge, U.K.: William B. Eerdmans Publishing Company.

Gold, J. (2012). *A natural alliance: Positive psychology, hope theory, and executive coaching* (Order No. 1516361). Available from ABI/INFORM Collection, 20–21.

Grant, A. M. (2002). *Towards a psychology of coaching: The impact of coaching on metacognition, mental health and goal attainment.*

Grant, A. M. (2011). Is it time to REGROW the GROW model? Issues related to teaching coaching session structures. *Coaching Psychologist, 7*(2).

Grant, A. M., Studholme, I., Verma, R., Kirkwood, L., Paton, B., & O'Connor, S. (2017). The impact of leadership coaching in an Australian healthcare setting. *Journal of Health Organization and Management, 31*(2), 237–252.

Hagen, M. S., Bialek, T. K., & Peterson, S. L. (2017). The nature of peer coaching: Definitions, goals, processes and outcomes. *European Journal of Training and Development, 41*(6), 540–558.

Hughes, R. K. (1998). *Luke: That you may know the truth.* Wheaton, IL: Crossway Books.

International Coach Federation. (n.d.). *Core competencies comparison table*. Retrieved from ICF - International Coach Federation: https://www.coachfederation.org/files/IndCred/ICFCompetenciesLevelsTable.pdf

Janes, J. L. (2016). *The sensemaking experience of newly appointed district teacher leader coordinators: A case study.*

Killian, C. (1996). Disciplines for the undisciplined. In M. Shelley (Ed.), *Deepening your ministry through prayer and personal growth: 30 strategies to transform your ministry* (1st ed.). Nashville, TN: Moorings.

Kimsey-House, H., Kimsey-House, K., Sandahl, P., & Whitworth, L. (2011). *Co-active coaching: Changing business, transforming lives.* Boston, MA: Nicholas Brealey Publishing.

Lewis, T. D., & Graham, G. (2003). 7 tips for effective listening. *The Internal Auditor, 60*(4), 23–25.

Louw, J. P., & Nida, E. A. (1996). *Greek-English lexicon of the new testament: Based on semantic domains* (2nd edition.). New York: United Bible Societies.

Mandal, A., Howard, T., & Antunes, D. (2009). Dynamic linkages between mental models, resource constraints and differential performance. *Journal of Strategy and Management, 2*(3), 217–239.

Manser, M. H. (2009). *Dictionary of Bible themes: The accessible and comprehensive tool for topical studies.* London: Martin Manser.

McFadyen, P. (1997). *Open Door on Mark: His Gospel Explored.* London: Triangle.

Mills, M. S. (1999). *The life of Christ: A study guide to the gospel record.* Dallas, TX: 3E Ministries.

Morris, R. (n.d.). *The blessed life: Simple secrets for achieving guaranteed financial results.* Life Outreach International.

Northouse, P. G. (2013). *Leadership: Theory and practice* (6th ed.). Thousand Oaks, CA: Sage Publications, Inc.

Norz, B. (2011). Coaching helps build great teams. *MLO: Medical Laboratory Observer, 43*(9), 28–29.

Oden, T. C. (1989). *Pastoral Counsel.* New York: Crossroad.

Palmer, S., & Whybrow, A. (Eds.). (2008). *Handbook of coaching psychology: A guide for practitioners.* New York, NY: Routledge.

Paralikar, S. (2018). A 'SIMPLE' and 'NICE' mentor who enables his mentee to 'GROW'. *National Journal of Integrated Research In Medicine, 9*(2), 94–96.

Passmore, J., & Oades, L. G. (2014). Positive psychology techniques - Active constructive responding. *Coaching Psychologist, 10*(2), 71–73.

Passmore, J., & Whybrow, A. (2007). Motivational interviewing: A specific approach for coaching psychologists In S. Palmer, & A. Whybrow (Eds.), *Handbook of coaching psychology.* New York, NY: Routledge, 160–173.

Patterson, K., Grenny, J., McMillan, R., & Switzler, A. (2012). *Crucial conversations: Tools for talking when stakes are high.* New York, NY: McGraw-Hill.

Phillips, T. (2011). Creating a coaching culture across a global sales force. *Strategic HR Review, 10*(4), 5–10.

Rees, P. S. (1974). Prayer and social concern. *Reformed Journal, 24*(1), 8–11.

Reissner, S. C., & Angélique, D. T. (2011). Power and the tale: Coaching as storyselling. *The Journal of Management Development, 30*(3), 247–259.

Richardson, L. (1998). Five-minute sales coaching. *Training & Development, 52*(9), 53–57.

Rosscup, J. E. (2008). *An exposition on prayer in the bible: Igniting the fuel to flame our communication with god.*

Bellingham, WA: Lexham Press.

Ryken, P. G., & Hughes, R. K. (2005). *Exodus: Saved for God's glory.* Wheaton, IL: Crossway Books.

Schemm, P. R. J. (2012). The writing pastor: An essay on spiritual formation. *Themelios, 37*(3).

Smith, A. T. (2012). Middle grades literacy coaching from the coach's perspective. *Research in Middle Level Education Online, 35*(5), 1–16.

Spurgeon, C. (2014). *Spurgeon Commentary: Philippians.* (E. Ritzema, Ed.). Bellingham, WA: Lexham Press.

Stoltzfus, T. (2005). *Leadership coaching: The disciplines, skills, and heart of a Christian coach.* Virginia Beach, VA: Coach22 Bookstore LLC.

Talbert, C. H. (2005). *Reading acts : A literary and theological commentary on the acts of the apostles* (Rev. ed.). Macon, GA: Smyth & Helwys Publishing.

Thomas, R. L. (1998). *New American standard Hebrew-Aramaic and Greek dictionaries: Updated edition.* Anaheim: Foundation Publications, Inc.

Torrey, R. A. (1906). *How to succeed in the Christian life.* New York; Chicago: Fleming H. Revell Company.

Tozer, A. W. (2009). *The counselor: Straight talk about the holy spirit.* Camp Hill, PA: Wing Spread Publishers.

Tyler, J. A. (2011). Reclaiming rare listening as a means of organizational re-enchantment. *Journal of Organizational Change Management, 24*(1), 143–157.

Ulrich, D. (2008). Coaching for results. *Business Strategy Series, 9*(3), 104–114.

Utley, R. J. (2000). *The first Christian primer: Matthew* (Vol. 9). Marshall, TX: Bible Lessons International.

Water, M. (1998). *Knowing God's will made easier*. Carlisle, UK: Hunt & Thorpe.

Wiersbe, W. W. (1992). *Wiersbe's expository outlines on the new testament*. Wheaton, IL: Victor Books.

Wilson, C. (2011). Developing a coaching culture. *Industrial and Commercial Training, 43*(7).

Wilson, C. (2013). *Teaching self-control: Coaching your child in constructive reactions*. Retrieved from Focus on the Family: https://www.focusonthefamily.ca/content/teaching-self-control-coaching-your-child-in-constructive-reactions.

Wright, T. (2004). *Luke for everyone*. London: Society for Promoting Christian Knowledge.

Wright, T. (2004). *Mark for Everyone*. London: Society for Promoting Christian Knowledge.

Wright, T. (2004). *Matthew for everyone, part 1: Chapters 1–15*. London: Society for Promoting Christian Knowledge.

Wright, T. (2004). *Matthew for everyone, part 2: Chapters 16–28*. London: Society for Promoting Christian Knowledge.

Wright, T. (2004). *Paul for everyone: The prison letters: Ephesians, Philippians, Colossians, and Philemon*. London: Society for Promoting Christian Knowledge.

9 781949 572452

CPSIA information can be obtained
at www.ICGtesting.com
Printed in the USA
FFHW011337240419
51959935-57377FF